The Official
ROCKY
Scrapbook

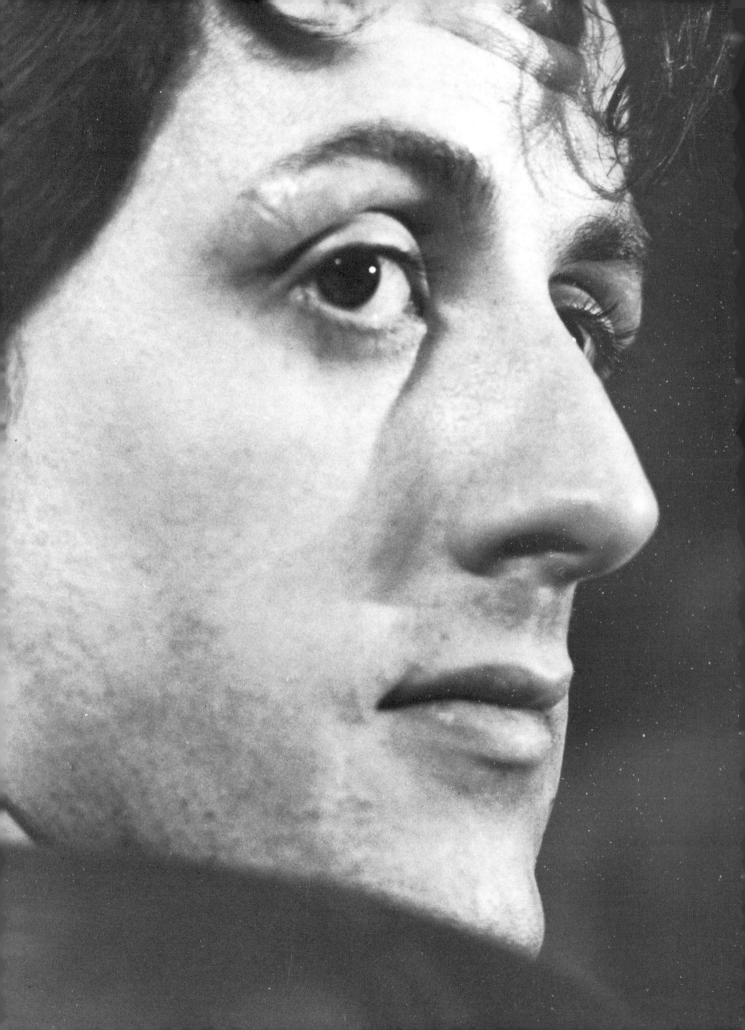

The Official ROCKY Scrapbook

by Sylvester Stallone

Grosset & Dunlap
Publishers   New York
A Filmways Company

To my wife, to my life, to my future strife.

Copyright © 1977 by Sylvester Stallone
All rights reserved
Published simultaneously in Canada
Library of Congress catalog card number: 77-77294
ISBN 0-448-14432-8 (hardcover edition)
ISBN 0-448-14433-6 (paperback edition)
First printing 1977
Printed in the United States of America

Contents

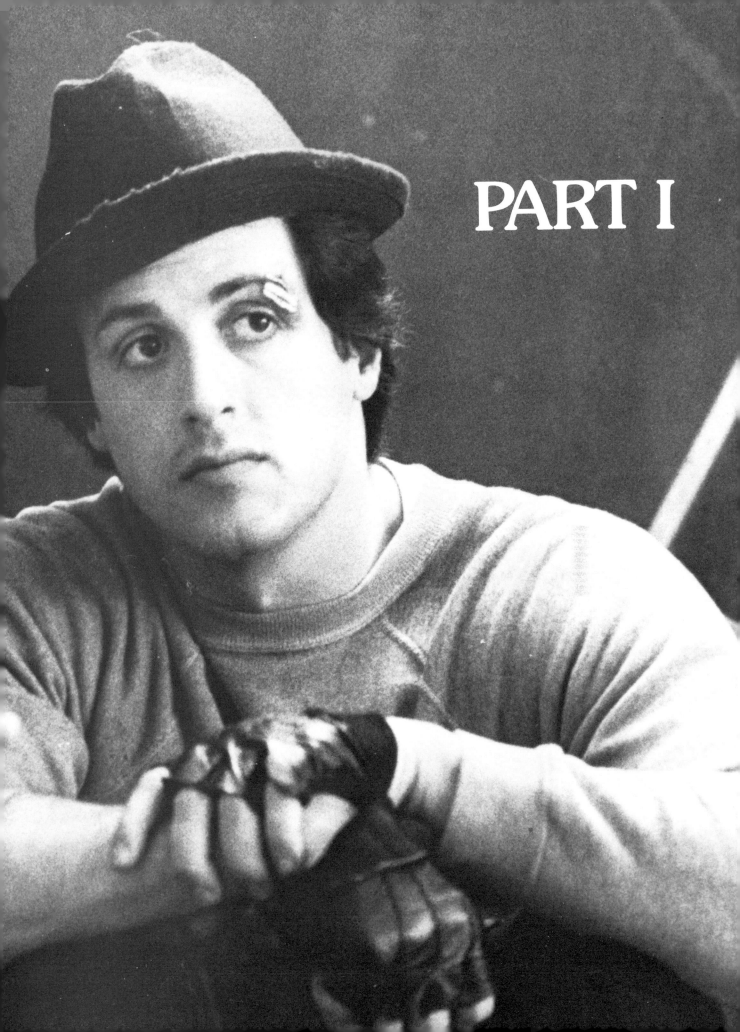

PART I

1. | I Discover Rocky Balboa

To tell you a little bit about myself, I'm not that much more exceptional than any other actor. I've always maintained that maybe I had something unusual, maybe I had something special that eventually I could sell, but the problem was finding someone who would buy that product—and that's exactly what it is: a product. If people think along heavily esoteric terms in which they are pure artists who won't ever sell out, they'll never make it because, unfortunately, the business revolves around the decimal point and the dollar sign; so you have to be artistic and commercial at the same time.

In 1969, I was about as inartistic and uncommercial as any human being could be. I had just come back from Europe where I had recently purchased a backpack and some walking boots. Of course, I had also just sold those after four days of ownership. Why did I sell them? Well, in 1969, it seemed to be the vogue for everyone in their late teens and early twenties to go out and hit the road and find themselves. Why should I be any different?

Even though I didn't have any idea of what I was searching for, I felt that hitting the road was easier than getting a job and somehow, it seemed to be in unison with the times. So there I was, backpack, stained dungarees, stiff undershirt, hair as greasy as a pork chop, walking my way through Europe, puffing along, living on the wind—probably the most boring existence on the face of the earth.

I maintained that routine for three days until finally I hitch-hiked a ride down to the Costa Brava in Spain. And there I was sitting on the sand, on a moonlit night, trying to pick up pieces of shell and with only a hunk of cheese that I had purchased as my total meal for the day. I lived on mussels for twenty pesetas and a piece of cheese—they call it cheese—that looked like a large hunk of dandruff.

With the crashing of the waves in my ears and the moon caroming off the water, it sounded and looked very romantic, but somehow I wasn't being overwhelmed by all this nature. If anything, I was beginning to suffer guilt complexes and a guilt reflex syndrome simply because I wasn't doing anything with my life. I was just becoming a movable statue. So, I sat up that night contemplating my existence, and the following morning as the sun was coming over the horizon, the sum total of all the wisdom of my life came to me in one big unexciting burst. "If you really want to find yourself, where do you look?" And the answer that came to me from the depths of my soul said, "Reach into your pocket, Sylvester, and grab your ass, because if you want to know where you are and who you are, you'll find it back there."

And lo and behold, the answer was right. I had found myself. So I jumped up, packed up my belongings and headed for the first plane smoking—in Zurich. I don't know why I went to Zurich but somehow I ended up there less than twenty-four hours later and I got on the plane for home. And I remember my arrival in New York simply because the headlines that day were scream-ing about some new revolutionary gathering place called Woodstock. I had no idea what Woodstock was. I thought perhaps Woodstock was an investment in a woodchuck farm. But anyway, Woodstock was the beginning of getting back to nature, getting back to honesty, getting back to roots. I guess we all were very excited about that prospect.

Tramping through New York, I didn't do anything exceptional. I found myself a fleabag joint to live in. I lived there for six days until my money ran out and I spent the next eleven days sleeping on a bench in the Port Authority Bus Station with other aspiring junkies, assorted street maniacs, and, every now and then, a budding artist of sorts.

I became an actor by chance. I had only been on stage when I was eight in a Cub Scout play about Smokey the Bear. I played the lower half of the bear. While in college I was cast in a play almost by accident, but it felt good performing and I had finally found something that was not illegal that I enjoyed.

I distinctly remember my first audition in New York. It was for a man named Sal Mineo. I was going out for this tough guy in a script he had, I think, recently optioned, called *Fortune and Men's Eyes* and the character's name was Rocky. Prophetic, wouldn't you say? So I auditioned for Rocky and Sal said "Well, Sly, you just don't intimidate me." I couldn't believe my ears. Not intimidate Sal Mineo? Sal Mineo was perhaps the size of one of my arms. So I proceeded to shove this stage manager around. I flipped over all the furniture and I leaped off the stage and grabbed him by his kerchief and said, *"Now* do I intimidate you?" I didn't intimidate him any longer. I terrified him and now he wanted to work with me even less. So that was my rather lackluster début in the New York world of theater.

After that major setback and I do say it was a major setback, because I believe we actors share the common dream that we'll walk into a studio or onto a stage and immediately the director will say "Ah, just the one I've been looking for!" Or, "Isn't he perfect?" Or, "My God, another James Dean!" (or some other thespian of great artistic proportions). Usually they told me, "Take a shower and get into another field of endeavor." That's when I began to cool on theater: after perhaps six or seven thousand rejections. And I mean classical rejections—the kind of rejections where I couldn't even get into the office. They'd say, for example, "Slip your picture under the door, Sylvester," and I'd slip my picture under the door. Ten seconds later, the picture would come out all wrinkled and with stains on it, and they'd say, "No sale." I had no idea what they were using the pictures for. And I had no idea of the face of my rejector. That bothered me. At least I would have liked to see the man say it to my face. Again, it was becoming a pattern where, after a while, I could build up immunities to rejection. What that developed in me was a sense of humor. I knew that if I didn't laugh a great deal about what was happening, I would surely explode. And as we know, we have enough exploding human beings in the world without my contributing to the problem.

By 1973, I would say I had been flatly rejected by every casting agent in every agency in New York City. I had already been signed with five agencies and had met with five failures at communication. They simply didn't seem to work for me. It was as though they had all been coached by the same dialogue instructor. They'd say, "Sylvester, whatever you have, no one seems to be in the market for. You are a unique case. You seem to require special handling. There is no call for your particular type." And you wonder why psychiatrists will one day inherit the world! They go around giving out bad advice, forgetting that many actors live on a precariously delicate glass ledge that borders between sanity and dangerous depression and rather than

Demonstrating the art of the long bomb in Switzerland.

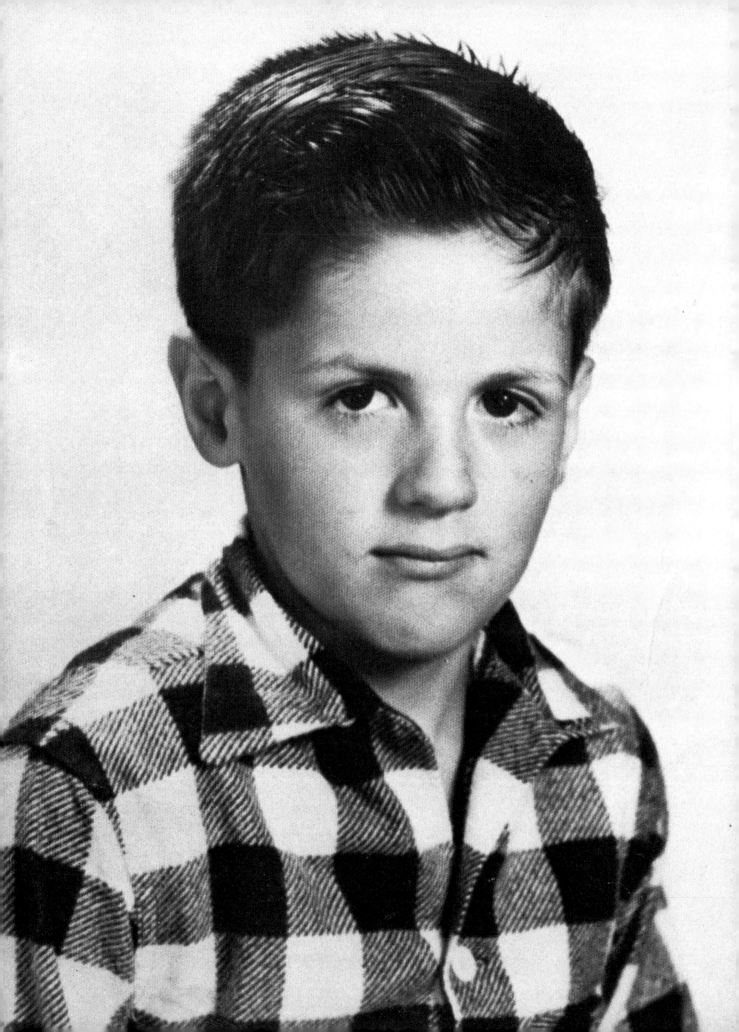

Manning the first illegal hamburger stand at
the American College.

Left: At the age of eight.

handling you in a gentle fashion, these people, these agents do things that only inflame the situation.

So, by 1974, I had already been employed as an usher, a fish-head cutter, a lion-cage cleaner, a basket boy, a bouncer chasing bums out of an apartment building, and had had other assorted jobs that I took just to leave my days open so I could circulate among the casting agents. I remember distinctly that at the beginning of 1974 I had decided that my New Year's resolution was that I had to find out if I had any other options in life. I recalled having seen several films—*Easy Rider* for one—which I felt that I could duplicate. I could make an inexpensive film and make it even more interesting and maybe as socially affecting as that one. I proceeded to buy a nineteen-cent Bic pen and a forty-nine-cent pad and with these two objects, I planned on altering my career.

I really was going downhill fast. I don't know if I was beginning to panic but I could definitely hear the wolf at the door. I knew my options were running out. I certainly could not go to medical school since I had hardly been able to get out of high school. And college—I don't know why they kept me there. I suppose they needed the tuition. Because college proved one thing (and I have said this before and I'll say it again): college proved that I could go for four years without having any brain waves or a single original thought. I believe the last place an acting student should be is in college. It just seems to be counter-productive to realism, the type of realism that he will eventually be asked to portray. But to each his own.

As I said earlier, I felt I couldn't do any worse than the *Easy Rider* script and perhaps I could do better. Well, lo and behold, I did do worse. I did so badly that I don't even think the script was worth training a bird on. I don't know whatever happened to it. I think it was called *Cry Full and Whisper Empty in the Same Breath* or some other pretentious title; but even though the script was bad, it gave me a sense of accomplishment. Here I had written one hundred and eighty pages of garbage but somehow that put the gears in motion and lubricated my creative self in such a fashion that I began to enjoy it. I began to see an accomplishment. All those hours I had spent going around to auditions and being flatly turned down, and here I had spent several days at home (however long it took to produce a script) and I was seeing a result. It was on the page. It might not have been classic prose but it was an accomplishment—a timeless accomplishment, an accomplishment that wouldn't dissolve. I could always say: *You see that? I did have dedication. I did sit down and I did complete a story from beginning to end. For better or worse, it's there.*

This was something new for me because I was a man who had never passed an English course in his life, a man in whom even the mention of a spelling bee would strike terror because I knew I would be the first one to bomb out and end up in his seat. And it's always that first one people snicker at, especially when you are asked to spell the word *car* and you ask the teacher to give you a hint. But I should jump ahead a year and a half.

By that time, I had completed eight screen plays and still had not sold any because they all reveled in pessimism. They were all drenched in negativism, nihilism, the idea that man is no good, and the Hemingway philosophy that every story should end in the death of its protagonist—its hero should go down in flames. Well, maybe it worked for Hemingway, but it sure wasn't paying my gas and electric.

By this time, I had completely given up my acting career. I had disassociated myself from thespianism in any shape or form.

One day—I don't recall exactly the month—I bought a can of black spray paint and blackened all my windows so I had no sense of time. I disconnected my phone. I disassociated myself from any communications with so-called friends and acquaintances and I only kept in touch with only one or two people that I could actually relate to, and that was simply to bounce ideas off of them.

Then I entered that subterranean world of writers, the world of fantasy, the world of mobile ideas in imagery. I continued to write tremendously fast. I remember I once wrote six half-hour television dramas in one day and one evening, in a matter of fourteen hours—so writing came fairly easy to me. I did not care if fifty percent of the first draft was rotten; I'd correct the mistakes later. It seems I had had all these fantasies percolating, incubating for years and now they all seemed to be coming out in one wave. . . . I still hadn't earned a cent.

I remember that it was around the end of 1974 and I had been in a film called *The Lords of Flatbush*. I received a few dollars for that which came in handy and I proceeded to buy a forty-dollar Oldsmobile, which Nature had painted rust. Very nice. Two-tone corrosion.

I threw whatever possessions I had—a beautiful wife, my voracious monster dog—in the car, and set out west. I would say the car broke down at least three thousand times on the way out here—about every mile—but it gave me a sense of pioneer spirit. At least I felt this was the way our forefathers had done it; and eventually, we made it to California. I don't know if it was prophetic but the car blew up on Hollywood and La Brea and

As Stanley Rosiello (*center*) in *The Lords of Flatbush* (*Henry Winkler is at right*).

Competing for the American College of Switzerland track team.

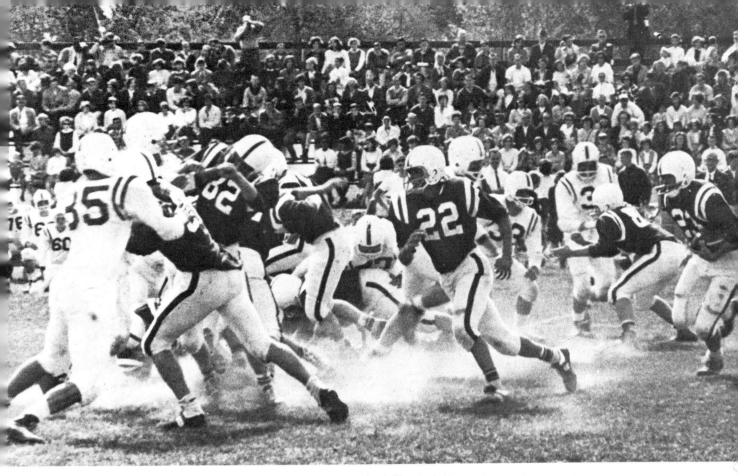

As fullback (22) on the conference-title Devereux–Manor Hall High School football team, Berwyn, Pennsylvania.

The football squad of the American College (I am number 44).

we gave it a decent burial not far from that spot.

After seven months in Hollywood, writing continuously, I concluded that the only difference between my West Coast and my East Coast existence was that on the West Coast, I was unemployed with a tan rather than with the sickly green hue that had followed me around during my New York days. Even though I was writing out here, all my scripts seemed to be entrenched in pessimism and again the Hemingway philosophy that all the heroes must die in the end and go down in the one big blaze of glory. Even though violence and degradation and whatever the sadistic vogue was—it seemed to change monthly—were selling, I didn't have a beat on it. I was writing things that I thought would definitely sell but no one was buying.

The turning point came without a doubt at my twenty-ninth birthday party. It was in July and I was sitting across the table from my wife who was growing wider with pregnancy and my dog who was eating his own fleas because we were so broke. My wife had purchased a $1.15 cake at a local store and we were looking at one another and talking. She was saying, "Make a wish," and I looked around and I wished I was out of this place so badly and I knew that the only way I was ever going to get out of this place was not through "physicalization" but actually through creative endeavor, dedication, discipline. Then I got a pang, I got a pang of fear, of fright, of uncertainty, knowing that the situation could only be getting worse. *It is getting worse; it is not getting better. I have a child on the way and there is nothing in the fire. I am going down for the third time. What am I going to do now?*

I've had these electrical jolts of paranoia several times before and every time they came on me, I would go to my writing table and scratch out a new idea. This time was no different. I made my excuses as soon as I had gorged myself on cake and ice cream which tasted as if it had been made by Dupont, and headed for my writing room, which was a folding table outside the garage. I was again hit with another jolt and that was the realization that all I had been writing had been trite, that it had been done before and I was simply yielding to a vogue. What did *I* really enjoy seeing up on the screen? I enjoyed heroism. I enjoyed great love. I enjoyed stories of dignity, of courage, of man's ability to rise above his station and take life by the throat and not let go until he succeeded. Yet no one was making films like that. "They" would call that corny, outdated, and thirtyish or a throwback to the forties or the unrealistic fifties. Well, not me. I knew I had a story in me but I didn't have any idea what the handle would be, where to fix my energies.

Through fate or whatever, I ended up at the Muhammad Ali/Chuck Wepner fight. Chuck Wepner, a battling bruising type of club fighter who had never really made the big, big time, was now having his shot. But the fight was not regarded as a serious battle. It was called a public joke. He would barely go three rounds, most of the predictions said. Well, the history books will read that he went fifteen rounds and he established himself as one of the few men who had ever gone the distance with Muhammad Ali and he can hold his head up high forever no matter what happens. I am sure that moment meant more to him than any money he could ever receive from fighting because now he had run the complete circle. This is why he had been training for thirty-four years.

That night I went home and I had the beginning of my character. I had him now. I was going to make a creation called Rocky Balboa, a man from the streets, a walking cliché of sorts, the all-American tragedy, a man who didn't have much mentality but had incredible emotion and patriotism and spirituality and good nature even though nature had not been good to him. All he required from life was a warm bed and some food and maybe a laugh during the day. He was a man of simple tastes.

The second ingredient had to be me, my particular story, my inability to be recognized. I felt Rocky to be the perfect vehicle for that kind of sensibility. So I took my story and injected it into the body of Rocky Balboa because no one, I felt, would be interested in listening to or watching or reading a story about a down-and-out, struggling actor/writer. It just didn't conjure up waves of empathy even from me and I was sure it wouldn't do it from an audience either. But Rocky Balboa was different. He was America's child. He was to the seventies what Chaplin's Little Tramp was to the twenties.

For the next three and a half days straight, Sasha, my wife, who had always done the typing, was called upon to go above and beyond the call of duty. I wrote and she typed. We had a two-person factory going. We'd watch the sun go up and the sun go down and we'd eat standing up and she would struggle and slap herself in the face at the typewriter to keep herself awake.

I don't know why we were pushing so hard. No one was asking for the script. I didn't have a producer giving me a deadline, but deep down inside I knew that something was brewing. There was heat. I knew that the time was now and that the quicker I got it out, the quicker it was going to be sold. It's as though the stars were aligning themselves for some great cataclysmic explosion and I wanted to be ready when it happened. . . . I told myself any lie to keep going.

Rocky says, "I'm no bum."

The script was done in three and a half days and I took it to my agent who felt very good about it. He took it to a man called Gene Kirkwood, a neophyte producer who had just been hired by the studios. He had no features under his belt at all. *Rocky* was going to be his first. So he took it to his heart. Then he took it in to the producers and the producers' response was also very good at first. They asked for several changes and they got them.

Every day, I was in conference with Irwin Winkler and Robert Chartoff, the producers, until finally the hour came when they said "Yes, we want the script!"

I said "Great!" And the sum of $75,000 was mentioned. This is a staggering amount for a man who has $106.00 in the bank and nothing coming over the hill. Zero.

I went home and I thought about it. I didn't tell my wife about it. I came back the next day and I refused it. The fee went to $125,000. When I heard that, I immediately got a migraine headache over my left eye—$125,000—no one in the world has that kind of money. They asked me why I didn't want to sell it. The answer was simple. I wrote it for me. *I* wanted to do it.

They replied that they would *love* me to do it—only I was not bankable; I was an unknown commodity. They felt that they should go with Ryan O'Neal, who enjoyed boxing, or Burt Reynolds or Paul Newman or Steve McQueen, or Al Pacino—or any one of the ten or fifteen major actors who are marketable, because I was about as marketable as tear gas. Nobody wanted me around but I wasn't about to let this thing go.

$200,000.

No.

$210,000.

No.

$235,000.

No.

You're crazy, Sylvester.

I know that, but it's incurable.

$245,000.

No sale.

All right, Sylvester. $255,000. That's American currency.

I went outside and I thought about it and I thought that I was losing my grip. But then something down inside, or wherever our real conscience lives, told me that the money meant nothing. *This is it. You're on the ride of your life. Don't let go because if you do, you're going to hate yourself for the rest of your life. The movie is about not selling out. The movie is about going the distance. The movie is about that million-to-one shot. Don't become a hack.*

Rocky daydreams.

Another consideration came into my mind and that was that I was no longer alone in this world. I was not the solitary man. I had obligations. I had a wife. I went home and I told her about the situation and that the money could probably buy us indefinite security and at least guarantee a substantial writing career, for in Hollywood, usually if you sell one script, you're bound to sell many, many more. The trick is getting that first one sold.

I'll never forget her response: "Go for it," she said.

The next day, the bid went up to $265,000 and I made a simple declaration to my agent and whoever wanted to hear, that I would sooner burn the script, that I would sooner bury the script, that I would sooner put the script out to sea and blow it up than to have anyone else play Rocky. "If the price went up to half a million, if the price went up to a million," I said, "No sale."

Finally, the producers swung over to my side and used their influence to convince United Artists to take me on. The script went to Arthur Krim, Eric Pleskow, Mike Medavoy, and all the upper echelon of the United Artists organization and finally it came down, the word from above, that it was a "go" for one million dollars. Not a penny more, not a penny less.

One million dollars!

2. The Preliminaries

If there was ever a script that was destined to cost more than a million dollars, *Rocky* was a prime candidate. One million dollars—no more, no less.

My deal now was to work solely for scale—not a penny more, not a penny less. I would have done it for an olive and a glass of water. The money meant nothing. It was the opportunity. And the producers offered me a percentage of the film, which I felt was quite extraordinary.

After an evening of celebrating with my wife, panic set in— again. I realized: *I have to make a movie, a movie that will rise or fall on my performance.* It was that simple. I'll report on the continuation of that moment of uncertainty later on because the real panic came to a head the first day shooting.

We set out to find a director, a director who had a street savvy, a man who could work under a tight schedule and for limited money and could inject the special energy that would be required to pull off this particular undertaking.

John Avildsen had had some difficulty in features before *Rocky* and that difficulty usually stemmed from a strong sense of independence and dedication to the project rather than to the commercial aspect. His famous quote was always: ''Great art never came through compromise.'' And he's a man who truly lives by that credo. It was funny though, because John Avildsen was a man for whom I had auditioned two years earlier for a bit

John Avildsen

role in a movie called *W.W. and The Dixie Dancekings* and I had even failed at that while in New York. Now here it was two years later, and *he* was directing *my* movie. The theater world is a small one.

While the producer and the director were busy hiring the necessary personnel to deal with the technical side of the filming, I began to submerge myself into the world of a boxer. I had a trainer named Jimmy Gambina who had been raised around fighters, had been with them all his life and he had the tough job of whipping me into shape. I had started lifting weights some years before because if I had to exist I did not want to exist as a paper-thin, droop-eyed kid from Maryland, which is what I was. Getting in shape meant getting up every morning at four o'clock, running, coming home at six o'clock. Going back to bed for an hour. Getting up at seven, eating a light breakfast, going to the gym, sparring all morning. Coming home, eating a heavy lunch, taking a nap. Getting up in the afternoon, having a massage. Then, a little later on, punching the heavy bag, the speed bag, jumping rope, pushups, running, calisthenics, stretching, and finally—hitting the showers. Hit the showers. That became one of my favorite phrases.

I didn't know how I was going to fool the public into thinking that I was a professional fighter with twelve to fifteen years' experience. It wasn't going to be easy because I couldn't even fool myself. I was clumsy. I couldn't hit the speed bag. My timing on the heavy bag was ridiculous; I continually sprained my wrist and bent my thumbs back and brought smiles to the faces of observing fighters. But I studied thousands and thousands and thousands of feet of fight footage and concluded that boxing is a muscular dance of sorts. You have a partner. You move around that partner and the objective is to move with the flow rather than against the flow; it's counterpoint, countermovement, counterbalance. In other words, boxing is merely a matter of geometrics and guts.

My second major problem was to find a partner, that is, a heavyweight champ, a man who could look like a fantastic athlete but also say the lines that would be required of this particular character who was named Apollo Creed.

At first we had professional fighters come in by the hundreds. Several times we had near-altercations in the waiting room as one fighter would look at another fighter and challenge him to a match right then and there. Some fighters had terrible damage—brain damage, that is—and were nearly unable to speak, while others were extremely glib but as soon as you gave them a script, they became timid. But my theory was, and still is, that fighters are performers. They love the public eye. Many of them are not as communicative as normal actors would be but they relate in their own way. They thrive on the adulation the way a performer does when he takes a bow after a performance. Notice the way a fighter reacts to a cheering crowd after a victory—it's quite similar.

At first, Kenny Norton was the prime target for Apollo Creed but Kenny has great size and since I am only five foot ten and one hundred eighty-five pounds, against a two hundred thirty-pound man like Kenny, it would have looked as though I were a middleweight.

After a week, we were getting desperate until by sheer fluke, the producer received a call from an agency saying, "Would you mind seeing one of our clients? His name is Carl Weathers." Well, Carl Weathers came into the office and by this time, I was tired. It was late at night. Carl was very exuberant. Of course, he would be; I mean, he was there for an audition. All I wanted was a cold compress and a place to lie down. Carl came in and told us how he was right for the part, and one thing was certain—he wasn't lacking confidence. He was asked to read the role of Apollo Creed opposite me. He had no idea who I was. He thought I was just some semi-literate office boy because I had submerged myself so far into the character of Rocky that I didn't exactly sound like your typical writer. I appeared to be the janitor's nephew who was just there to do the windows or take out the trash; in other words, I was a yawning basket case.

Jimmy Gambina

Carl read the part and I thought he was good, but he turned to the producers and complained: "Oh, I would have done much, much better if you had given me a *real* actor to read with."

I looked at myself. I had always considered myself a real actor, but Carl had no idea who I was so I decided to play along with the ruse and I said, "You're right. You should have a real actor but since we're here, why don't we box? Let's see what kind of body you have." So Carl took off his shirt and needless to say, he has probably one of the finer bodies in the world; it's perfectly sculptured—a natural body that was perfect for the champion. He's a born natural, in fact. Then he began to box. Carl is not a fighter; he is an actor but he has a great background as an athlete and he began to dance around the office, just lightly throwing jabs out. Then he began to tag me. And he was hitting me in the forehead. And I'm there suffering brain damage helping this man audition for *my* movie. Well, I start chopping back but then I decide to call it a day before we end up playing the major portion of the movie from the intensive care ward at Mount Sinai Hospital.

Carl was a winner. Carl got the part.

So now my schedule was beginning to read like this: training, sweating, getting beat up in the morning; and working on casting and production in the afternoon. The training went pretty smoothly until the first day I got into the ring with a legitimate heavyweight. This man, who I thought possessed a normal brain and knew I was an actor, cocked back and cracked me over the heart. I was still adjusting my headgear when he hit me.

The pain was probably the most intense I had ever felt. I thought one of my lungs had been punched out through my body and was lying somewhere on the gym floor. I became very angry with this man. I wanted to kill him. So, I proceeded to chase him around the ring, not knowing anything about boxing; just merely on the attack. I finally caught up with him on the ropes and he was hitting me, nine, ten, twelve times in a row but I caught him and inflicted what I considered justifiable damage. Then I went home and was not able to get out of the bed for close to four weeks. That was my indoctrination into the world of boxing.

Back at the office, we were having difficulty casting the role of Adrian. My concept of her was as someone very thin and birdlike, with long brown hair, and the role had been given pretty much to Carrie Snodgrass. But Carrie Snodgrass's agent was holding up the paper work over some price disagreement. Meanwhile, I had remembered Talia Shire from *The Godfather* and asked that she come in. Talia Shire came in. She wore glasses, her hair was short and dark; she was almost the opposite of the way I had pictured Adrian. She came in with enthusiasm and gave one of the finer improvisational readings I had seen since working on the film. And at the very end of the improvisation, she reeled back and gave me a couple shots in the jaw, playfully, as though she were a fighter. I felt that she had achieved near total control over the character even in this short span of time and I wanted her badly and I screamed and yelled and made everyone around me uncomfortable until finally they said, "Okay, you've got her!" which was an incredibly great coup for us all.

Then came the brother, Paulie. Paulie was a difficult role. Here I needed a man who had a temper that would rival a moray eel's. But I also needed a man who could be a world-wide symbol of the blue-collar, disenfranchised, left-out mentality, a man who feels life has given him an unfair amount of cheap shots but really it hasn't—it's only in his imagination. He has made his bed and now he has to sleep in it.

Burt Young is a puzzle of a human being, a walking dichotomy. He's a brute of a man, capable of inflicting incredible

Burt Young

Talia Shire

punishment because of his natural strength and skills as a professional fighter who has fought and remained undefeated. Yet the
flip side of Burt Young is that he possesses a sensitivity and a
gentleness that staggers me whenever I meet the man; he has a
humbleness, a quiet side, and great intelligence, for he also has a
writer's mind. I think of Burt Young just as I do of myself—as a
writer who acts. When Burt agreed to do the part of Paulie, I
knew that we were just about home.

INT. ROCKY'S APARTMENT—NIGHT

Rocky returns home and enters his apartment. After turning on the light, he flips on his RECORD PLAYER. He now feeds the turtles.

ROCKY
Look who's home!

Rocky notices two telegrams laying inside the threshold. He approaches them with a sense of awe. He opens and reads one. Settling on the bed, he reads the other.

A KNOCK is HEARD. Rocky opens the door. Mickey Goldmill, the gym owner, stands framed in the doorway.

MICKEY
I seen the light. I figure somebody was home.

ROCKY
Hey, Mickey—Whatta ya doin' here? Here, sit down.

Rocky tosses soiled clothing off a mangled armchair.

ROCKY
Best seat in the house—Hey, Mick, this is too much.

MICKEY
How do you mean?

ROCKY
I'm usta seein' ya at the gym, but seein' ya here, in my house, it's kinda outta joint.

By the manner in which Goldmill listens, it is obvious something important is preying on his mind.

Rocky is slightly uncomfortable, almost embarrassed at having outsiders see how he lives.

ROCKY
Had to come on the maid's night off, right?

MICKEY
Listen, Rock, you're a very lucky guy.

ROCKY
Yeah.

MICKEY
What's happened is freak luck.

ROCKY
Freak luck for sure.

MICKEY
Look at all them other fighters. Real good boys. Good records. Colorful. Fight their hearts out for peanuts . . .

But who cared? Nobody. They got it shoved in their back door. Nobody ever give them a shot at the title . . . But you gotta shot.

ROCKY
Freak luck is a strange thing.

Mickey does not hear. His attention is drawn to the turtles.

MICKEY
Whatta' those?

ROCKY
Turtles . . . domestic turtles.

MICKEY
Anyway . . . I'm here tellin' ya to be very careful with this shot. It don't come again. You need the best trainin' and advice you can get.

ROCKY
I'll try an' get it.

Mickey looks hard into Rocky's eyes.

MICKEY
You need a manager. An advisor. Fifty years in the business, I am. I've done it all, there ain't nothin' about pugilism that ain't up here.

ROCKY
Fifty years, huh.

MICKEY
[*stronger*]
Fifty years. My rep is known. A good rep can't be bought, but I don't have to tell you that.

ROCKY
How 'bout a beer?

MICKEY
No . . . Rocky, d'ya know what I done?

ROCKY
[*uneasy*]
What?

MICKEY
[*driving each word hard*]
I've done it all.

ROCKY
Yeah.

MICKEY
I've seen everything. Believe what I'm tellin' ya . . . I even seen Firpo knock Dempsey outta the ring in 1923, September 14.

ROCKY

Ya got a good mind for dates.

MICKEY

New Year's Eve, 1952 . . . I seen the only time Jake LaMotta's legs give way under a Danny Nardico right . . . Jake the Bull . . . And, kid, I think Marciano woulda beat the whole German army in his prime. Christ, I remember that bastard. Stay outta small planes.

Rocky points to his most prized possession.

ROCKY

There's his picture.

MICKEY

Y'know, ya kinda remind me of the Rock. Ya move like 'im.

Mickey has rung the bell. Nothing could please Rocky more than being compared to his idol.

ROCKY

Really think so?

MICKEY

Ya got heart.

Rocky shifts against the wall and lowers himself into a crouch.

MICKEY

Christ, I know this business. Rocky, I even remember when the middleweight jinx began . . . startin' with Stanley Ketchel. Shot dead in 1910. Shot he was. Harry Greb and Tiger Flowers dyin' from bad eye operations . . . quack bastards. Billy Pape, suicide in '36. Kid McCoy in '40 . . . Al 'Bummy' Davis, a personal friend, almost let me handle him once. Killed in a Brooklyn bar in '45 . . . Cerdan, Sands, Don Lee, Bobby Horn takin' by way of freak accidents. Turpin shot in '66. Rocky, I got knowledge. I wanna give that knowledge to you.

Rocky rises and absently begins toying with turtles.

MICKEY

[*continuing*]

Respect, I always treated ya with respect.

ROCKY

I didn't need no respect.

MICKEY

I always knew ya had heart. I give ya a locker when ya needed it. I never charged ya.

ROCKY

Ya gave it to Dipper.

MICKEY

[*almost begging*]

Kid, I'm askin' man to man. I wanna be ya manager.

ROCKY

The fight's set . . . I don't need a manager.

MICKEY

I know more than anybody in Philly. You can't buy what I know. Ya can't. Ya need critical eyes . . . eyes like mine. I've seen it all!

ROCKY

Mick, I gotta take my shot alone. Can ya understand that?

MICKEY

Please, kid.

ROCKY

[*tightly*]

I needed ya help 'bout ten years ago, when I was startin'. . . . But ya never helped me none. Whatever I got, I always got on the slide. This title shot's no different. I didn't earn nothin'. . . . I got it on the slide.

Mickey drops the ashtray and kneels to pick it up

MICKEY

If you wanted my help, why didn't ya ask? Just ask.

ROCKY

I asked, but ya never heard nothin'!

MICKEY

Fifty years in the business, an' I never had a winner. Rocky, I'm seventy-nine. Your shot is my last shot.

Rocky is choked and goes into the bathroom and closes the door.

Mickey struggles to his feet and, like a beaten man, leaves.

Several moments later Rocky steps out and lowers himself into bed. Springing up a second later, he runs outside.

EXT. STREET OF ROCKY'S APARTMENT—NIGHT

Rocky races up the block toward the shadowy and hunched form of Mickey Goldmill. Way in the distance, we see Rocky stop the old man beneath a street lamp. He places an arm around his shoulder.

Carl Weathers

Next was Burgess Meredith. His was about the most coveted role in the entire script. Nearly every mature actor in Hollywood wanted that role and I only wish I could have used them all because I felt that any of them would have done a creditable job. But it appears that Burgess Meredith worked just a little bit harder for he wasn't taken merely on his reputation. He came into the office like anyone else and he performed so well that it left little doubt that he would take the role to his heart and that he would do the excellent job that he did do.

Now with the majority of the cast assembled, I could begin working on perfecting my fighting skills, so that I could at least fool somebody. Carl and I would arrive at the gym every morning and fight for several hours. After a week of this, John, the director, decided it was time to bring in a professional choreographer—a stunt man, if you will.

Well, the first stunt man that came in seemed very enthusiastic; he said that he had fought Marciano—not *fought* Marciano but sparred with Marciano—and that he had done several of the famous fight films. I was impressed. But he had no idea what I was talking about when I told him I felt the fight had to be not your usual Hollywood slam-bang slugfest but instead a poetic ballet, a geometric movement where the punches would be placed in such a mathematical fashion that it would end up being controlled choreography—so that it would bring about the desired response from the audience.

Most stunt coordinators come in two, or maybe three days before the fight and they just move through the motions and when you're filming, you cut and readjust. If you make any mistake, you've only shot ten seconds, fifteen seconds, maybe thirty seconds at a time and you can cut and then move the shots around. Well, this had to be different.

I felt that we had to go fifteen rounds nonstop. We had to know exactly what we were doing every minute for forty-five minutes. That is the time of a heavyweight fight: forty-five minutes of boxing, fifteen minutes of rest. I didn't know how to do this at first and then John Avildsen, the director came to me and said, "All right, Sly. Why don't you put it down on paper? Why don't you actually choreograph the fight in your mind?" A simple but brilliant idea. I got a tape recorder and I proceeded to envision myself as Howard Cosell, sitting ringside and commenting on the fight between Apollo Creed and an underdog southpaw named Rocky Balboa. And it went something like this:

"And the fighters move from their corners. They touch gloves. The champion is moving smoothly. He glides to his right. Jab, jab, jab! A rapierlike jab. Folks, he may not be in the best shape

Burgess Meredith

he's ever been in but he's moving smoothly. The plodding challenger looks ineffectual. Ah! A hook by Rocky! Another hook! They didn't even come close. The champion is laughing. He circles to the right now. Jab, jab, jab! Not even bothering to use his right. He may just win this fight on jabs. He backs Rocky into a corner, he's moving in—doesn't even seem to be worried about the challenger. He throws a left; it misses. A right; it misses. Rocky *explodes* with a left—the champion is down!''

I proceeded to do that for all fifteen rounds and I gave it to a typist. She put it on the page and I handed it to one of the stunt men. I said: ''I would like you to work with us as we do this entire

Mickey instructing Rocky on the value of getting angry.

fight, punch by punch as it is on that page." They said it couldn't be done—it would look stupid—and they refused to do it. I got mad at them and they didn't like me; they called me a prima donna and they left.

Another set of stunt men came in. They felt that the film was going to be a lackluster affair—a B or C product, if you will—and they weren't interested. So finally I went to the director and said, "Let *me* do it. I'll do it. What the hell! I choreographed it on the page. Maybe I can do it for real. Carl and I will work together. We'll become the Fred Astaire and Ginger Rogers of the pugilistic world."

From that day on, Carl and I knew that the success of the movie was going to be determined by whether the fight had the emotional impact it was intended to have. Nearly every day Carl would fly down from Oakland and we would work the equivalent of four to five hours a day. In the final analysis, the ring fight in the movie runs just over nine minutes. And for all the hours that we put in training, it broke down to thirty-five and a half hours of boxing rehearsal for each one minute of fighting, whereas in most fight films you spend perhaps an hour or two hours rehearsing each round—and that's it at the most.

We knew we had to make the fight at least as good as the finest boxing match ever choreographed and we were going to try our damnedest. Besides, we had nothing else to do. We watched every fight film from beginning to end and also every authentic boxing movie made. The fight films went as far back as the early 1900s, the first being the Jack Johnson/Stanley Ketchell match, and we finally ended watching the great Muhammad Ali/Joe Frazier Manila struggle of 1975.

At night, I met with a new chore that I had no idea would be as time-consuming as it was destined to be. It was called "the wonderful world of rewriting."

For those interested in speed writing, *Rocky* was about 122 pages long and went to more than 330 or 340 pages of revisions and we barely altered it from the original concept when all was done. But that's the way movies get made and that's part of the business—"the wonderful world of rewriting." Someone once said (and it still holds true), "One does not write; he rewrites."

Meanwhile Carl Weathers and I had been beating each other into flesh jelly as the starting date approached. On December 4th, I was scheduled to fly to Philadelphia with my wife and Butkus, my 145-pound bull-mastiff who was also to be in the movie. We were to begin shooting on the 5th.

I want to sidetrack here for a moment and tell the story of Butkus. Originally in the script, Rocky owned a scruffy, down-

One of the few times I actually connected.

and-out fleabag of a dog that only could be owned by a devout animal-lover such as Rocky was. Well, a down-and-out, fleabag dog, trained and for rent by a movie company did not come cheaply and since our budget did not allot us money for even a feeble hamster, much less a trained dog, the producers drew me aside and said, "Sly, would you happen to have an animal of your own?"

I said, "I have a thing called Butkus that's a throwback to the Stone Age."

"Well, will he follow you around? Will he do tricks? Will he act like a stage dog, a movie dog?"

I said, "I'll ask him."

And Butkus became a costar.

Returning to our travel plan, I was supposed to fly to Philadelphia on December 4th with my wife and animal. But a great wind of humanity blew over me and I thought that putting the dog in the cargo compartment for six hours alone, cold, suspended thirty-five thousand feet in the air, would be cruel and maybe would warp his walnut-sized brain. So I suggested that my wife, the dog, and myself take the train—the train, the great American symbol of strength, of uniformity, of basic ingenuity.

Though everyone I met said, "Do not take the train," I laughed. What did they know? The train, though a forgotten mode of transportation, would be peaceful. I would have three or four days to study my script, relax, and by the time I got to Philadelphia, I would not be suffering from jet lag. Instead I would be well rested, well rehearsed, and ready to go.

The first night on the train, I thought I was going to kill myself and my dog and leave Sasha a widow. They stuck us in a compartment perhaps the size of a coffin built for two; and I don't know how anyone could ever sleep while being rocked, with the clacking of tracks and whistles blowing while obese stewards banged their bodies against the door, and when one room flushed its toilet, the water drained out of your commode.

To compound matters, the dog refused to go to the bathroom. The only time this train stopped was at 3:30 in the morning. I would set the alarm, run outside in my underwear, knee-deep in snow, and beg the dog to evacuate. Several times, I found myself squeezing him in a bear hug, trying to assist nature—but to no avail. My dog set a new transcontinental record. He did not go to the bathroom for three and a half days and thirty-four hundred miles. But he did release the pressure in the form of gas bombs. These blasts of gas would come thundering across the room and nearly drive me and Sasha into convulsions. I almost considered whittling a cork and blocking up the foul passage.

Somewhere near Chicago, I was shaving and the train must have hit a rough spot of track because all the water shifted out of the basin and fell onto the carpet and across my luggage and drenched the floor. I didn't think much of it at the time and went to bed and the dog went to his usual resting spot in the corner, which happened to be on top of the wetness. I got up three hours later, called my trusty dog to my side, and noticed that all the red dye from the floor had been transferred to his body and would not come out. All I could think about was how or where were we going to film Butkus when one side looked like a beige bull-mastiff and the other like a cheap, red-headed fright wig.

For eleven hours, Sasha and I in a six-by-four-foot room scrubbed the dog until, to this day, he will attack at the sight of a bar of soap.

We managed to make it to Philadelphia without committing collective suicide but I was more tired than I had been in many months of training.

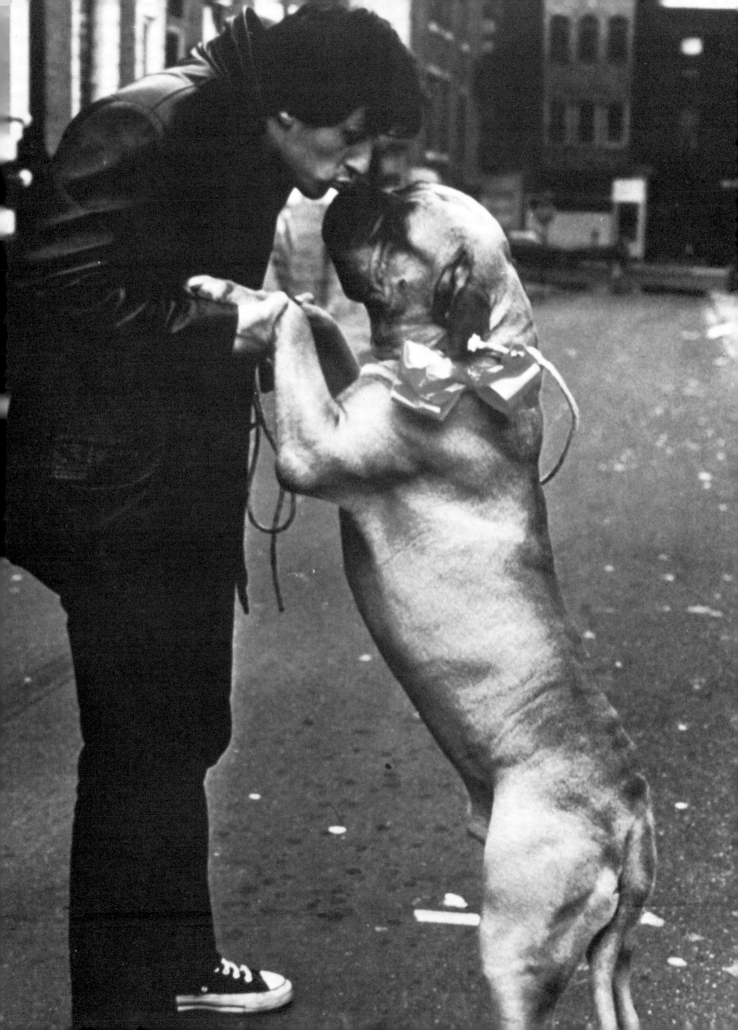

3. ROCKY Becomes a Reality

The morning of December 5th arrived with nearly zero-degree weather. I had been unable to sleep the night before, anticipating the day ahead. I had gone over every scene in my mind; every piece of dialogue; every bit of business. I knew it was under control.

At four o'clock, the make-up man, Mike Westmore, a gifted craftsman, knocked on my door, staggered across the room—no one was meant to get up this early—and proceeded to apply the make-up that he had built, piece by piece, for my face. It was brilliant. On several make-up tests before the filming, I had gone home in full battle make-up and never once did anyone detect that it was not for real.

While Mike applied the make-up, I turned on my tape recorder and listened to "positive thinking" speeches I had had recorded earlier—speeches dealing with acting and imagination and the ability to take control if anything goes awry. I needed these "positive thinking" speeches because my contract stated that I could be fired within ten days if for any reason they—the producers or United Artists—objected to my acting, did not like my moral conduct, or if I did anything peculiar like eloping with Butkus.

Now the knock (the one I had not been looking forward to, in some respects), from the assistant director, filled the room.

It was time.

As I went downstairs and was loaded into the trailer, I had never been so cold. I saw my wife there, wrapped up in everything that wasn't nailed down. If she were strong enough, I am sure she would have put a couple of armholes in the queen-size mattress and worn it as a vest. To say it was cold is a gross understatement.

On the ride over, I discovered more about myself than I had in the past nine or ten years. A great thud of responsibility came over me. I knew that if I failed, the movie would fail. Since I was in at least ninety percent of the scenes, no one other than myself could be blamed for the movie's shortcomings. And I knew that if this movie bombed, it was doubtful that any other unknown would get such an unusual opportunity.

I felt the trailer veer to the curb and I knew we were at the site. The streets were deserted except for a few professional losers who made their living in the gutter and somehow seemed only too perfect for the setting.

I was feeling apprehensive, knowing that in five minutes the movie was going to become a reality. No more talking, no more campaign speeches and promises, no more jokes about how great it was all going to be. This was the moment. I was standing at the starting line. And I still wasn't ready.

I asked if everyone would leave me alone. I watched Sasha step outside and close the door and then I stood in front of a small mirror. I studied my scarred eye make-up and the stocking cap pulled tight over my head and the filthy sweat suit with "The Italian Stallion" etched in grease pencil across the back and wondered if I could submerge myself far enough into this fantasy, into this character, to make the audience, and me, believe.

I still wasn't certain I could do it until there was a knock at the door and the assistant director said, "Okay, Sly, we're ready."

For some reason I turned around and said, "Sly went back to California. He told me to take his place. Yeah, the name's Rocky, how ya doin'?"

And he said, "You're on, Rock."

I stepped outside and the wind really sliced into my face but it felt good. It was the perfect environment for Rocky's training. The first scene was the running toward City Hall and traveling toward the exhausting mountain of steps that would cause Rocky to buckle in pain.

I felt confidence in myself. Now I wanted to feel total confidence in my director. I knew John Avildsen had to believe in the project as much as I did. But I've always felt that talk is very cheap. Simply because a man says he is dedicated to a project and you can feel his verbal enthusiasm, you don't know his real

Director John Avildsen coaching me on an entrance.

strengths or weaknesses until the moment of truth arrives.

I looked around for John Avildsen and expected him to be sitting in his director's chair discussing the next shot with the director of photography. I almost stepped on John Avildsen because he was lying in the gutter with a director's viewfinder lining up the shot. Looking down at this man lying on the freezing cement, I knew now that John Avildsen was totally involved.

On December 5, 1975 at 4:35 A.M., Rocky Balboa crawled off the pages of a script and was born.

Because of our tight budget, the filming in Philadelphia went at a bullet's pace. I spent the first day running nearly nineteen miles to get all the necessary training footage. The second day, we had some additional ideas for training, such as running past City Hall again, and Independence Hall, and leaping over benches and going past familiar Philadelphia landmarks. So I spent that day running eleven miles.

But something I hadn't planned on happened. I developed a case of shin splints. This happens when the muscle pulls away from the shinbone after you run too hard and too long on a hard surface such as cement or asphalt. It's a problem I've had since high school.

About six o'clock at night on the second day, while running past the Schuylkill River, my legs buckled for the first time in my life. I could not run anymore. I lay down and instead of having someone come over and say, "What's wrong? Let me put you in a truck and we'll take you to a doctor." Or "We'll get you a

(Text continued on page 42)

EXT. ATOMIC HOAGIE SHOP—NIGHT

Two blocks further on Rocky passes an all-night sandwich shop. In the window hangs the sign, "The Atomic Hoagie Shoppe, Inc." . . . Out front are several young men and women. They are much too young to be hanging out at this hour . . . A BOY with a badly chipped tooth beckons to Rocky.

CHIPPED TOOTH
[aggressively]
Hey, man—Buy us some wine, man.

ROCKY
No wine.

CHIPPED TOOTH
C'mon, man, it's cold.

ROCKY
No wine.

CHIPPED TOOTH
Yo, Rock, Gimme a dollar.

ROCKY
Why?

CHIPPED TOOTH
[sarcastically]
'Cause we dig ya, man . . . Gimme a dollar.

ROCKY
No dollar.

CHIPPED TOOTH
Hey, give Rocky a dime.

YOUNG MAN #2
. . . How come?

CHIPPED TOOTH
So he can call all his friends.

ROCKY
[mildly embarrassed]
. . . That's an old one.

CHIPPED TOOTH
Buy us some Thunderbird, man.

Rocky ignores the statement and faces a very young girl who is smoking and leaning whore-like against the wall.

ROCKY
Is that Marie? . . . Marie, ya brother know you're hangin' out so late?

The girl, MARIE, assumes an indifferent attitude, attempting to impress her friends.

MARIE
. . . Screw you.

ROCKY
[awed]
What'd you say?

MARIE
. . . Screw you, yoyo.

The gang laughs. Angered and shocked, Rocky grabs her arm.

ROCKY
Did these guys teach you to talk dirty? Huh?

MARIE
Hey . . .

ROCKY
What?

MARIE
Stuff it, man!

ROCKY
[shakes her]
Don't you never say that . . .
[to the gang]
. . . You guys talk like that in front of a little girl . . . You guys are scum.

CHIPPED TOOTH
This is our place, dig!

ROCKY
Don't ya never come round this girl . . . Go home.

YOUNG MAN #2
This is our corner, man! You go, chump!

Rocky moves forward and they scatter . . .

CHIPPED TOOTH
[backpedaling]
We'll kill you man . . . We gotta gun.

ROCKY
Pull heat on me? . . . I'll dent ya face!

Rocky leads the girl away.

ROCKY
'Cause that's the way guys are . . . They laugh when ya talk dirty. They think ya cute for a while, but then ya getta reputation an' watch out. Nobody's ever gonna take ya serious. Ya get no respect . . . I gotta use a bad word . . . Whore. You'll end up maybe becomin' a whore.

MARIE
C'mon, Rocky, I'm twelve.

ROCKY

That doesn't matter . . . You don't really have to be a whore, just act like one an' that's it.

MARIE

What?

ROCKY

Yo, a bad reputation . . . Twenty years from now people will say 'D'you remember Marie?' 'No, who was she?' 'She was that little whore who hung out at the Atomic Hoagie Shop.' 'Oh, now I remember!' . . . See, they don't remember *you,* they remember the *rep.*

Rocky and Marie exit the dark school yard . . . Standing in the shadows of the building are three young muggers. The light from their cigarettes flares red in their faces.

The muggers pace Rocky across the street and follow them down the block . . . Rocky sees them and stops and faces the three. The muggers pause and study Rocky from a distance of twenty yards. Rocky gives a loud boxer's snort, wipes his nose with the side of his thumb and rolls his shoulders . . . The muggers are intimidated and slowly peel off and meander away.

Rocky turns to Marie who has been standing behind him.

ROCKY

[*points down the block*]
. . . That's your house, ain't it?

Marie nods.

EXT. STREET—NIGHT

Rocky is walking the young girl home . . . They are presently cutting through a dark public school yard. They pass through the beams of light cast off by weak flood lights located at the top of the school building. The atmosphere is somewhat eerie.

ROCKY

How come ya wanna hang out with those guys? They teach ya bad things.

MARIE

I like 'em. If you don't you can f———.

ROCKY

Hey! When I was your age, there was only one girl who talked like that in the whole neighborhood.

MARIE

[*bored*]
. . . Yeah.

She attempts to light a cigarette . . . Rocky nonchalantly tosses it to the ground.

ROCKY

Make your teeth yella . . .

MARIE

I like yella teeth.

ROCKY

Makes your breath like garbage.

MARIE

Maybe I like garbage.

ROCKY

Nobody likes garbage . . . Anyway, this girl with the dirty mouth wasn't bad lookin', but the guys wouldn't take her out for any serious datin'.

MARIE

Why?

ROCKY

[*continuing*]
Listen, I hope ya don't . . .

MARIE

I won't.

ROCKY

What was I gonna say?

MARIE

Ya hope I don't keep acting like a whore or I'll turn into one, right?

ROCKY

Ya, somethin' like that.

They exchange smiles and Marie moves away. Rocky has made an impact on her life.

MARIE

Goodnight, Rocky.

ROCKY

'Night, Marie.

She takes a few more steps and pauses again.

MARIE

. . . Screw you, Creepo!!!

The girl runs to her house as Rocky looks on in dismay.

ROCKY

[*walks off*]
. . . Yeah, who're you to give advice, Creepo.

(continued from page 39)

rubdown to remedy the situation," John Avildsen runs over and says, "Film it! Film that agony, it's real. Can you crawl, Sly?"

"Sure I can crawl, John, I can crawl right over to you and strangle you with both hands."

Anyway, John was great. He took advantage of the situation and filmed me grabbing my legs like a dying swan and though we never made use of the scene in the final film, it gives one some idea of how the director was able to utilize a situation that might have become a real plus factor for the film had we decided to go with it. The only reason we didn't go with the collapsing scene was simply because the film was running too long.

The third day consisted of my scenes with Adrian. I spent the entire day in the pet shop with her, talking to birds and wondering if this was really a pet shop or a front for some numbers racket. It was hard to imagine why anyone would want to buy a fish lying on its side covered in green moss; or why all the hamsters were walking on three legs or missing a tail or looking around for a razor to slit their own throats. It had to be the most depressing pet shop I had ever seen.

Yet, in those surroundings, Talia Shire's character fit so perfectly. Her characterization was an absolute reflection of the dismal, depressing atmosphere of that pet shop. Considering the circumstances, I was amazed at Talia's concentration. She had just had a child two months before and it was extremely difficult for her son to be separated from her at such a young age particularly since the child had had serious difficulties in earliest infancy. Yet we spent our time between shots walking around the block and getting to know one another and getting the feel of Fishtown— that was the nickname of the neighborhood of Kensington in which we were shooting—into our sensibilities.

Seeing Talia against the Philadelphia background made me doubly sure that she was very right for this role. Now if *I* could only live up to my expectations.

That night was spent solely in walking up and down the streets and trying to get her into my apartment. After about twenty takes (because of camera difficulty), we began to lose our concentration. The cold was beginning to settle deep in our bodies and we knew if that happened it would definitely affect our acting. To compound the problem, a group of about five guys, who were stoned, huddled on the perimeter of the production area yelling challenges to me. Such things as, "I can take him … You know, you don't look so bad to me … OK, man, let's go! . . . Let's throw hands, man!" I tried to ignore this for about twenty minutes but it got to be too much. The weather was making me cold and these guys were making me hot. It was becoming a difficult situation under which to work.

When the cameraman paused to reload, I went over to the biggest one in the group, the man with the big mouth. He sneered at me with whatever teeth he had left hanging from his gums but didn't say anything. I said, "Hey man, you know, I see you got great potential."

He said, "What's that mean?"

"Come 'ere, I want to shake your hand." So he stuck his hand out and I grabbed it quickly and started to compress all his knuckles into one.

I knew he wouldn't scream or make any gesture of pain because his friends were around and I asked him, "Why don't you come up there and act with me? I think you've got star quality. Come on. Come on, we're good friends. We're shaking hands, aren't we? I'll tell you what I'll do. I'll go over there and get the cameraman to come over here and film you and your friends doing a love scene."

I walked over to the cameraman and was going to tell him the situation and have him spin the camera around toward the group but suddenly they were gone. Who knows? That group may have been the seventies' answer to the Dead End Kids. But no one will ever know now.

On the fourth day, a major problem struck. The actor playing the loan shark, Mr. Gazzo, was just unable to complete the role.

I went to a phone booth and called my friend, Joe Spinell. I had worked with Joe for a few days, on *Farewell, My Lovely* and I felt that he had just the right qualities to pull off the loan shark character. Initially in the script, I had pictured the character an older man, a more patriarchal type, but later on, I felt that perhaps he should be a member of Rocky's peer group. Fate was with us again because Joe Spinell came on a moment's notice. The director loved him; he jumped into the character as though it had been tailored for him, and played it with such ease and such superiority that at times I found myself wondering if I should ask him for a loan.

Joe Spinell was amazing. One of his major contributions came during a major scene in which he was arguing with Rocky. Joe had a minor asthma attack but, rather than breaking the scene, he pulled out his inhaler, gave himself several medicinal blasts, and continued on without ever losing the beat, which added a naturalness to the scene that made it very memorable. Joe Spinell alias Joey Chuckles—my friend.

Moving back to California I thought would be a great change because the entire crew and all the actors had been worn down by the hectic pace set in Philadelphia. But if anything, the pace

Practicing love scene with Tally.

(continued on page 46)

INT. ROCKY'S APARTMENT—NIGHT

Rocky and Adrian enter his one room apartment . . . She is nervous and taken aback by the bleakness of the room . . . Everything is worthless . . . Rocky goes to the ice box.

ROCKY

Would you like a beer or somethin'?

ADRIAN

. . . No thanks.

Adrian looks at the mirror above Rocky's dresser. She sees a high school photo of Rocky. He once was handsome and smooth-faced . . . Rocky steps up behind her and his face is reflected in the mirror.

He turns on his cheap RECORD PLAYER . . . He reaches into the turtle bowl.

ROCKY

Here's the guys I was tellin' you about
. . .

        [grabbing a turtle]
. . . This one is 'Cuff' an' the other's 'Link.'

ADRIAN

D'you have a phone?

ROCKY

        [slightly embarrassed]
I had it pulled. People callin' all the time. Who needs it . . . Who d'you wanna call?

ADRIAN

My brother. I want to let him know where I am.

ROCKY

D'you really wanna call?

ADRIAN

Yes, I do.

ROCKY

You sure?

ADRIAN

Yes.

ROCKY

Why?

ADRIAN

I think he might be worried.

ROCKY

I'll call your brother.

Rocky flings open the window and bellows like a foghorn.

ROCKY

        [continuing]
!!Yo, Paulie . . . Ya sister's with me! I'll call ya later.

Rocky closes the window and faces the woman . . . She is not smiling. She looks frightened.

ROCKY

        [continuing]
What's the matter? Ya don't like the apartment?

ADRIAN

It's fine.

ROCKY

It's only temporary.

ADRIAN

It's not that . . .

ROCKY

What's the problem? You don't like me . . . Don't like the turtles . . . What is it?

ADRIAN

I don't think I belong here.

ROCKY

It's okay.

ADRIAN

No, I don't belong here.

ROCKY

It's all right . . . You're my guest.

ADRIAN

. . . I've never been in a man's apartment before.

ROCKY

        [gesturing]
They're all the same.

ADRIAN

I'm not sure I know you well enough . . . I don't think I'm comfortable.

ROCKY

Yo, I'm not comfortable either.

ADRIAN

        [standing]
I should leave.

ROCKY

But I'm willin' to make the best of this uncomfortable situation.

Adrian moves to the door . . . Rocky intercepts her.

ROCKY
[*continuing softly*]
Would ya take off your glasses?

ADRIAN
[*dumbstruck*]
What?

ROCKY
The glasses . . . Please.

Rocky removes her glasses and looks deeply into her eyes.

ROCKY
[*continuing*]
. . . You got nice legs.

ADRIAN
[*timidly*]
. . . Th-thank you.

ROCKY
Do me another favor?

ADRIAN
. . . What?

ROCKY
Could ya let the hair down?

ADRIAN
Why are you doin' this?

After a moment, Adrian lets down her hair . . . She is becoming rather pretty.

ROCKY
A movie star.

ADRIAN
Don't tease me.

The woman melts into the corner and begins lightly sobbing . . . Rocky steps forward and fences her with his arms and body.

ROCKY
I wanna kiss ya . . . Ya don't have to kiss me back if ya don't feel like it.

Rocky softly kisses the woman . . . Her arms hang limp. He puts more passion into the kiss and she starts to respond. Her hand glides like smoke up his back. She embraces his neck. The dam of passion erupts. She gives herself freely for the first time in thirty years.

(continued from page 43)

was accelerated in California. Twelve-, fourteen-, sometimes eighteen-hour days became routine. John's hair had gone to nearly all gray hair in a matter of twenty days. Chartoff and Winkler had been losing weight because not only had they invested their time in the film, but they had also put up a completion bond. This meant that if the film went over schedule, the costs wouldn't come out of United Artists' pocket, but out of their own pockets, which also meant they would have to mortgage their homes and possibly end up with less than when they started.

But me—I had nothing to lose, so I was calm. I shouldn't say *calm* because I was beginning to separate myself from the crew. I noticed a growing disenchantment between me and several of the technicians mainly because I and all the actors were driving very, very hard to make this film the *best* that it could be. Our careers were on the line. They would go on to other films but *us*, this was *it!*

As a matter of fact, several of the men disliked me so much that they took their names off the credits before the film had even been completed. Now they are considering going to court to get the credits back. . . . Good luck.

If there was any one asset to the making of this movie and bringing it in on time, it was that we stuck almost religiously to the script, deviating only when absolutely necessary. For example, the only scene that I ad-libbed was the scene where I come out of the bathroom and yell at Burgess Meredith, my manager, for not having had any faith in me ten years earlier and ask why did he have to wait until we were both broken down and useless to come to my aid.

After filming in the apartment for two weeks, the gloominess of it, the futility of it all, had so gotten into my brain that I felt a need to editorialize coming on. I didn't know when it was going to happen but I knew it was coming. Something that couldn't be written on the page, something that had to come out. Originally the scene was supposed to end on a very soft note. But when I went into the bathroom, I caught a glimpse of my face in the mirror—this filthy, spotted mirror—and I grabbed the doorknob and it was covered in gray slime and there were defecation and years of wretched living plastered on the walls. When I came out of the bathroom, I knew this was the moment.

The director let it roll and it came out without any control. I turned to John Avildsen and he had water in his eyes. I turned to the camera operator and he gave me the "okay" sign. I turned to the sound man and I noticed that he was scratching his head; "I think the batteries are dead."

Rocky speaking with Cuff and Link.

It took us nearly twelve different takes to regain the energy that had been in that initial scene. Luckily John didn't get frustrated and hung on until he was satisfied that we had captured that all-important statement on the soul of Rocky Balboa.

On the last day of work in Rocky Balboa's apartment there was a love scene between myself and Talia. I noticed while kissing her, that she wouldn't lift her lips up and I was trying to be romantic while using my chin as a crowbar to pry her face up towards mine. Perhaps it enhanced the scene but I was beginning to wear out the skin on the right side of my chin, so I asked her exactly what the problem was. And after eight hours of kissing, she looked at me with those soulful eyes and said, "The reason I didn't want to kiss you is I have a terrible case of the flu."

The next thing I knew, I was in a doctor's office with needles sticking into me and tubes in my nose and visions of *Rocky* just rotting away on a doctor's table. All those hours of training turning into sickly green flab and I would be unable to be very convincing in the next scene because the following day was the training montage.

The training montage was something that I had been building toward for six months. I knew I would have to do what every fighter must to get himself in peak condition but I wanted to do it in even a more exaggerated form. So when it got to the part of throwing the medicine ball, I had Jimmy Gambina, my trainer, heaving the ball so hard that I expected my liver to come out and fall to my feet—and so did everyone else. But I think that kind of pain was necessary for it to register as real. We transferred the camera into the ring to film the pushups. It had been written as "Rocky does several two-handed pushups." But something crazy happens every time that camera rolls and before I knew it, I was flying from one hand to another doing an exercise that no boxer in his right mind would ever do; and I continued to do it. The next day I wished my shoulders belonged to someone else because I think I inflamed every joint in my body. It was worth it, but I never did it before or after.

Moving into the meat house for the pounding of the slabs of beef, I felt to be a real challenge. The beefs were used simply as a metaphor for the fighter's point of view while training. In other words, his opponents become nameless meat—indifferent, meaningless, dangerous meat. We spent approximately fourteen hours in the meat house. Jimmy taped my hands in such a fashion that I thought it would protect me against any broken bones while hitting the carcasses. But after eight hours, the cold penetrated the bandages and hitting the meat finally caused me

to crack a knuckle and drive it back into the middle of my hand. To this day, I still haven't seen it. But again, it was worth it. Hell, I've still got nine other knuckles.

Many people have mentioned to me that the most exciting part of the training montage is the sprint along the pier culminating in the ascent up the steps. The sprint along the pier was done while in Philadelphia. It was just before the shin splints set in and I felt as though I couldn't give this particular run the burst of speed required to make it as dynamic as I had hoped it would be. But as I've related before, amazing things happen when that camera begins to roll, and I felt my feet moving so fast that I thought I was going to topple forward and scrape my teeth along the asphalt until they were nothing but stumps. I actually felt myself losing control, losing balance. But after several trial runs, my body fell into the rhythm of the sprint pattern and we didn't have any trouble; so we moved on to the museum steps. At the steps, it had been my original intention to pick up my dog, Butkus, and go sprinting up the steps with him to show how much Rocky had increased his strength. But after carrying Butkus fifteen or so steps I knew that if I tried to carry him much farther, I would be playing the rest of the movie from Dr. Wong's Hernia Ward in Wisconsin or wherever. So, for the sake of sexual preservation, we decided to give Butkus the morning off to window shop.

Before I move on to the final fight scene, there are two incidents I would like to recount. One is the ice-skating scene. I think this is a classic example of invention coming out of necessity. I had written the ice-skating scene so that Adrian and I were skating along on the ice with 350 to 400 extras, on a very crowded Thanksgiving night. I thought it would give some feeling of embarrassment that Rocky and Adrian were such awkward skaters and we'd have all of the instructors and dance couples sliding past. But the day before we were ready to shoot, Irwin and Bob, the producers, pulled me into the office and said, "We're having a slight problem in the budget."

"Well, what's new," answered John.

"We're going to have to do with a few less extras than we'd planned."

I said, "All right, how many do we get? Two hundred?"

"A little less, Sly."

"One hundred and fifty?"

"Go down."

"Seventy-five?"

"How about none, Sylvester?"

This was quite a comedown from four hundred, so I thought

maybe we should set the date scene in the desert or in a rowboat somewhere where extras weren't necessary. But after several conferences with the producer and the director, we concluded that the scene might become even more dramatic with Rocky and Adrian alone on the ice. We proved we were right because the scene is infinitely better minus the distraction of three or four hundred extras trying to upstage one another.

And now the second incident—from the "I wish I had rewritten that scene" department. It was the scene where Burt Young, through his frustration, grabs a baseball bat, threatens his sister and then threatens Rocky with annihilation if he isn't given some part to play in this heavyweight championship. All I remember is Burt, this powerful hunk, coming at me with a baseball bat and having him smash this lamp, and then come down and smash the table (which was a real table) and real china, several inches from myself and from Talia's head.

Well, Burt was getting a little frustrated that day and very hot because the temperature in the room was, I would say, perhaps 105 or 110 degrees. And around the fifth take, I could see that the bat was inching closer and closer to my face. I didn't know if this was a subconscious death wish or whether Burt was trying to add a bit of improvisational realism to the scene at the expense of my skull.

I remember that when the bat was descending for the last time I blamed myself for not having written the scene with a small chiffon pillow instead of a sawed-off baseball bat. We live and learn though.

It was the morning of the big fight and we had advertised in the newspaper and on several radio stations that if you came down to the L.A. Sports Arena, you would be given a free chicken dinner if you would participate as a ringside spectator for the afternoon. Needless to say, that morning we had nearly four thousand people to witness the Apollo Creed/Rocky Balboa championship fight.

I was in my dressing room getting garbed when I heard that Joe Frazier, our special guest, had arrived and was in the dressing room next to mine. Everything was falling into place and this came as a great relief because by this time in the filming, everyone was on the verge of applying for a lifetime scholarship to a madhouse, and no one knew how we were going to get through this fight alive. So the fact that the pieces were coming together made me think a miracle was about to happen.

Disaster struck first in the form of a bathrobe. I had asked the wardrobe department to design a robe in maroon and yellow satin that would say "The Italian Stallion" across the back and

I'm trying to convince Frazier I don't want to fight him.

(continued on page 52)

49

EXT. ICE SKATING RINK—NIGHT*

(This is the scene as originally conceived. In the movie, however, the Instructor became an attendant whom Rocky bribes in order to walk with Adrian as she skates on the deserted after-hours rink.)

Rocky watches as Adrian slips on a rented pair of skates.

ROCKY
. . . Don't ya need to go to some special school to work with so many animals?

Adrian shakes her head no.

ROCKY
[continuing]
Sorry, didn't hear ya.

ADRIAN
. . . I only went to high school.

ROCKY
How d'ya like workin' with the puppies?

ADRIAN
. . . Fine.

ROCKY
How 'bout the snakes?

Adrian does not respond.

ROCKY
[continuing]
Scary?

ADRIAN
Not really . . . Can I ask you a question?

ROCKY
A question? . . . Absolutely.

ADRIAN
Why do you fight?

ROCKY
'Cause I can't sing or dance.

Adrian smiles and walks to the ice . . . Rocky follows.

EXT. ICE SKATING RINK—NIGHT

Rocky has followed Adrian onto the ice. He has never been on ice in his life. He wears street shoes and shuffles along.

ROCKY
Where'd ya learn this?

ADRIAN
My brother taught me.

ROCKY
Paulie! No kiddin' . . . Like I was sayin' before, fightin' use to be tops with me, but no more.

A thin graceful INSTRUCTOR in a bulky turtleneck unhappily eyes Rocky sliding along in street shoes.

ROCKY
[continuing]
All I wanted to prove was I weren't no tomato . . . That I had the stuff to make a good pro.

ADRIAN
And you never got the chance?

ROCKY
I ain't cryin' . . . I still fight. Do it like a hobby.

The Instructor glides over and makes a grand sweeping slide in front of Rocky.

INSTRUCTOR
[overbearing]
If you want to remain on the ice, put on skates.

ROCKY
[smiles]
Yeah, I'll be off in a minute.
[to Adrian]
See I'm a southpaw an' most pugs won't fight a southpaw . . . Southpaw means lefthanded.

They move away from the Instructor who reddens.

ROCKY
[continuing]
Things probably worked out for the best, right?

ADRIAN
But you never had a chance to prove yourself.

ROCKY
Absolutely.

Rocky removes a crumpled photo from his wallet.

ROCKY
[continuing]
That's me fightin' Big Baby Crenshaw. I lost, but it's a nice picture, don't ya think?

Adrian does a slight turn and Rocky has to speed up and nearly falls.

ROCKY
[*continuing*]
. . . I hit hard, real hard, but I'm a southpaw an' nobody wants to fight a southpaw so—

The irate Instructor speeds over and purposely stops in such a manner that sprays ice on the front of Rocky's pants.

ROCKY
[*continuing*]
You're great . . .

INSTRUCTOR
Either put on skates now, or get off the ice . . . Do it or I'll have you ejected from the rink, fella.

Rocky ignores him and slides off with Adrian . . . The Instructor is outraged.

ROCKY
Y'know how I got started in the fight racket?

ADRIAN
By accident.

ROCKY
My ol' man who was never the sharpest told me—I weren't born with much brain so I better use my body.

For the first time, Adrian laughs.

ROCKY
[*continuing*]
What's funny?

ADRIAN
My mother told me just the opposite. She said, 'You weren't born with much of a body, so you'd better develop your brain.'

Rocky laughs.

ROCKY
Sure we didn't have the same mother an' father?

The couple pass close to the angry Instructor. Rocky sees the Instructor is ready to hassle them again . . . Just as the Instructor is closing in and about to speak, Rocky looks straight ahead, but gives the man a casual straight-arm . . . The Instructor lands on his butt. Adrian never notices the maneuver and she and Rocky glide off.

Rocky realizing he can't win.

The Official ROCKY Scrapbook

Paulie turns Rocky into a billboard.

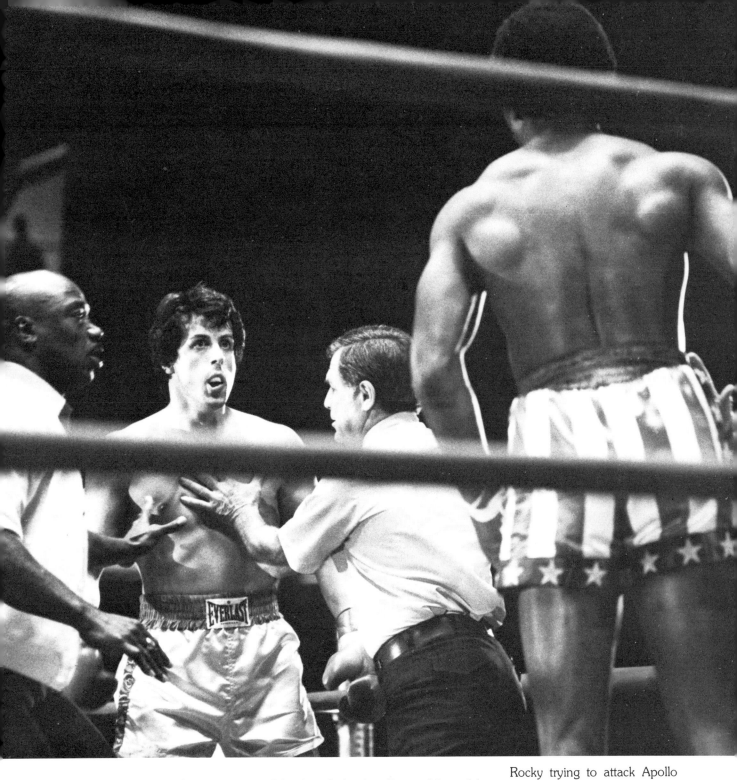

Rocky trying to attack Apollo after the bell.

ing life except me because now I had to fight Apollo and I could feel the adrenalin building up. Even though we had rehearsed for many, many months, I had never felt the excitement and the nearness of battle the way I felt it at that moment.

Carl leaped into the ring with great flair and jumped around. Then he stripped off his George Washington outfit and did his Yankee Doodle thing, which really sent the crowd into a frenzy. Several people threw paper cups and other assorted debris into the ring and everything started rolling.

4. The Big Fight

We had designed this fight to go fifteen rounds. It wasn't the type of thing where we would stop after ten seconds and then set up. John Avildsen had located six cameras around the ring knowing full well that Carl and I were prepared to go fifteen rounds—nonstop if necessary—to get the actual heat of battle. The only reason we would have to pause would be for make-up corrections, as both of our faces began to take on the brutalization of a heavyweight fight.

As the fight announcer came to the center of the ring, I noticed something was wrong. Someone was missing. Then it dawned on me; Joe Frazier was not there. I asked John where Joe Frazier was and he asked his first assistant director and the first assistant director asked the second assistant director and finally it came back that poor Joe had been sitting in his dressing room for nearly five hours waiting for his opportunity to come on stage and everyone felt that he was most likely very mad by now, and no one wanted to be the fool to go in there and have his spine tied into a square knot.

Finally someone summoned up the courage to go and tell Joe he was on and we continued to make our movie.

The crowd was beginning to get restless. They had consumed their free chicken dinners, burped, and were beginning to toss bones and chicken wings at Carl and myself. The audience was definitely split into two camps, one for Rocky and one for Apollo,

and they made their opinions known.

At the bell, I saw Carl move out of his corner with much more speed than he had in rehearsals and I felt myself moving much more aggressively than I ever had before. We began to lash into each other with a sort of controlled vengeance. The crowd was screaming because they were not certain if we were half-real, half-fake, or exactly what the situation was. Carl was driving punch after punch after punch into my face and the people in the audience was reacting as I hoped they would. They were becoming extremely frustrated by Rocky's futility, and I had the rare experience of witnessing my nose swelling in stages.

As planned, I lured Carl into my corner and caught him with a left hook and knocked him to the floor. The place went berserk. More chicken bones rained down from the rafters, cardboard tops sailed across the room, people screamed, people spit. They were beginning to get unruly, or maybe just human.

Carl got up and continued to fight. He completed the round by driving me into my corner and breaking my nose and then the pro-Apollo fans began to throw even more chicken bones at the pro-Rocky fans. The fight went along smoothly except for, I'd say, three major incidents. One involved my father who I mentioned before was playing the timekeeper. His job was to follow the choreography which I had written out for him and to ring the bell exactly at the moment specified. Otherwise Carl and I would continue to dance around out there throwing punches at random and, both of us being somewhat aggressive personalities, would inevitably break something and shut down production.

Into the fifth round, I felt myself being backed into the ropes by the champion and Carl was unleashing hell on my face and I knew that, after the fifth jab, a right cross would follow—and then the bell. I counted: one, two, three, four, five and here would come the right cross . . . bell. No bell!

Carl threw another right hand.

Bell?

No bell.

Rather than have this scene wasted by jumping up and yelling "Cut!" I decided to move to the center of the ring and give my father time to regain his senses and ring the bell before Carl and I commenced to killing each other. Carl started shooting lefts at me and I started throwing hooks at him and he caught me with a right on the nose that I thought was going to plaster it against the side of my face. I got mad and grabbed Carl in a clinch and shoved *him* back and we were getting into the heat of battle when I circled around towards the timekeeper and yelled over my shoulder, *"BELL!"* hoping that it would be undetected by the camera.

I yelled a second time, *"BELL!"*

No bell.

Finally, I turned around and yelled into my father's face, "What are you? Deaf? Did I fly you out here to get me mangled?"

Then *he* got very upset since he was suffering public embarrassment and yelled back. "Just mind your own business. You fight and I'll ring the bell," he said and angrily rang the bell.

Rather than have my father climb into the ring and have a fist fight with me, I thought it would be better left alone. So I yelled and carried on for a few more minutes to let off whatever steam I had built up. John really needed this family feud, right? But what I didn't know was that the audience was also getting into the heat of battle and they were being whipped into a frenzy.

The second incident occurred when Carl and I decided to improvise just one small boxing segment—a series of missed blows which I would duck under and then come up and catch the champion with a hook. One improvisational movement caused Carl to miss and he broke his thumb. He was in great pain for the rest of the fight. As a matter of fact, we were both in great pain for the rest of the fight simply because the gloves that we were wearing are called "Casanova" boxing gloves. These particular boxing gloves are outlawed in the United States because they are lethal. But I wanted them because of their sleek appearance. Even a near miss, a flick of this glove, can split open an eye, bust a nose, or rearrange your bridgework.

The third and most serious incident of the fight occurred during the final round. After Carl and I exchanged a heavy barrage of hooks and jabs and crosses, we fell into each other's arms and he yelled, "Ain't gonna be no rematch!" And I yelled back, "Don't want one!" Now the way it was written in the script was that Carl, of course, gets the decision and he is carried out on top of his adoring public and Rocky, to his surprise, is carried out by *his* adoring public. We had hired stunt men to play the individuals who would hoist us up and carry us out of the arena while we were surrounded by the extras but the scene did not go according to plan. As Carl was picked up and carried out of the ring, I saw several hundred people converge on him and I could see hands groping up toward him and fists lashing out and the man that played his trainer, Tony Burton, and his corner men were also being punched and jabbed. And then it was my turn to go into these—how should I phrase it?—over-zealous *fans*?

As I was being carried along, I felt a fist bury itself in my kidneys and I turned around and I saw this maniac staring at me with his eyes wide open and spinning. I went for him but he disappeared in the crowd and I turned around and saw another guy pulling back to take a cheap shot.

Even Burt Young was being harassed by some of these people. In those few minutes, the crowd had inflicted more pain on Carl and myself than all the training and the four days of fighting combined.

So for the sake of self-preservation, it was John's idea to have a unanimous decision to end the fight in the ring, which again I think was a stroke of fate, simply because the fight and its impact are so much more interesting with Adrian fighting her way through the crowd of selected extras to come into Rocky's arms. And for the first time he is able to say "I love you." And she is also able to say "I love you" for the first time. The audience feels that these two individuals have reached the apex of their lives at this particular moment. They can go no higher.

And that is what the movie was *really* all about. Two individuals—half people—two half people coming together making a whole person. Two individuals seeking love, seeking dignity, and finding courage along the way. The way my wife's love gave me strength.

And what were the ingredients for their success? Just two, love and loyalty. And I have found, since *Rocky* has now become a beautiful thing of my past, that those two elements—love and loyalty—whenever applied to *any* desire in life, will take you farther up the steps to your goal than any other fuel I can think of. Without love, loyalty, desires, passion, courage, dignities, faith, beliefs and all the other ingredients that go into making the human soul something so elevated that only God knows its limits, we are only shells bobbing aimlessly in a calm sea of mediocrity. . . . And if you can figure that out, please write and explain it to me because you're a better man than I am.

Friends during lunch breaks.

Sasha and I.
(Photo by Sasha Stallone)

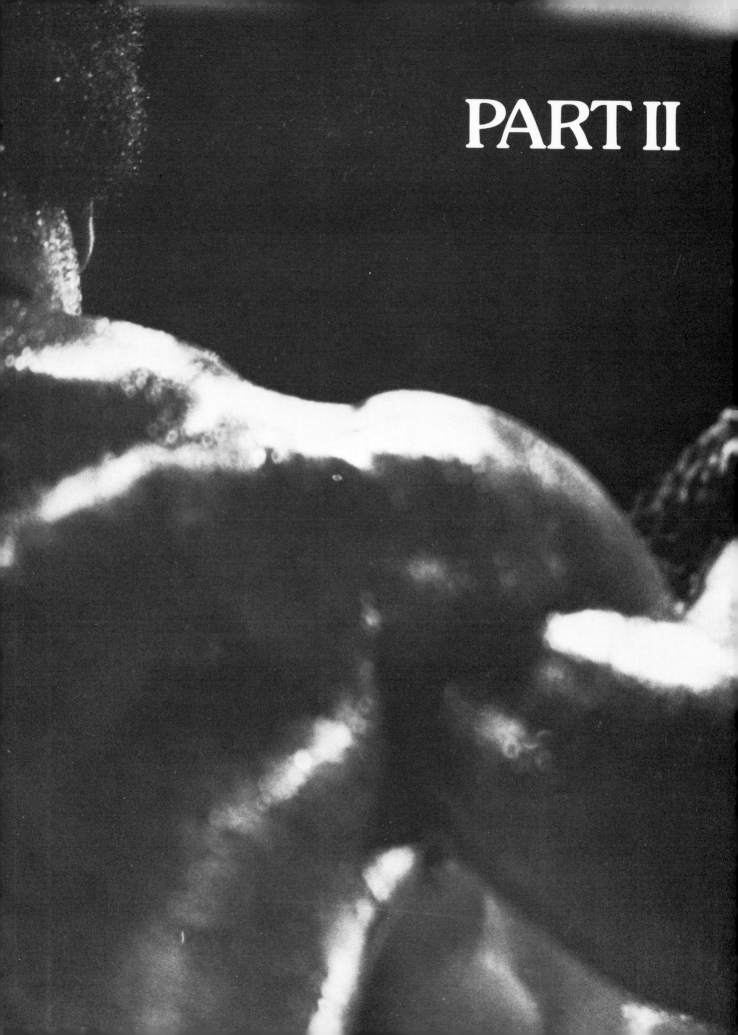

PART II

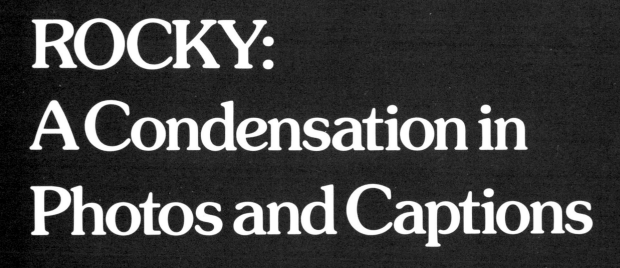

ROCKY:
A Condensation in
Photos and Captions

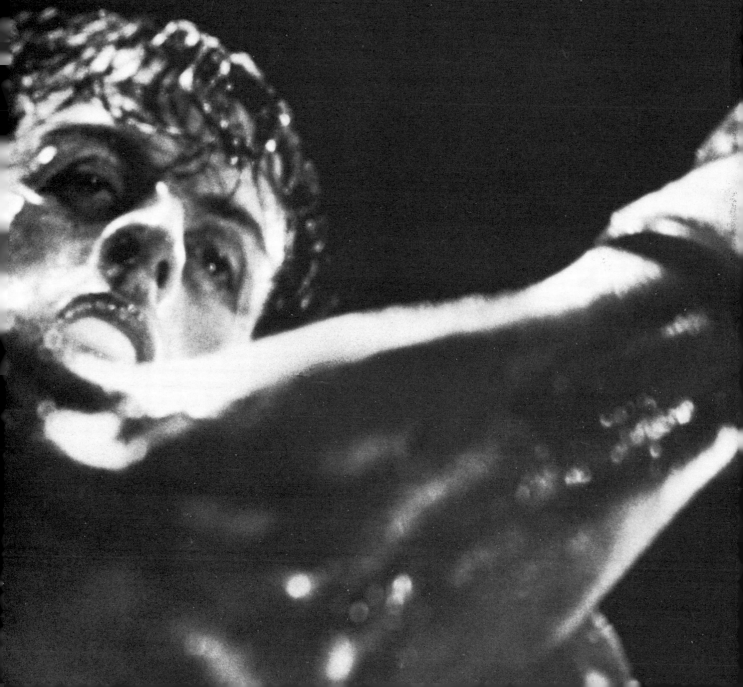

Rocky in the meathouse.

Paulie (Burt Young) threatens
Rocky for not giving him a job.

Practicing the meat
punching scene with Burt Young.

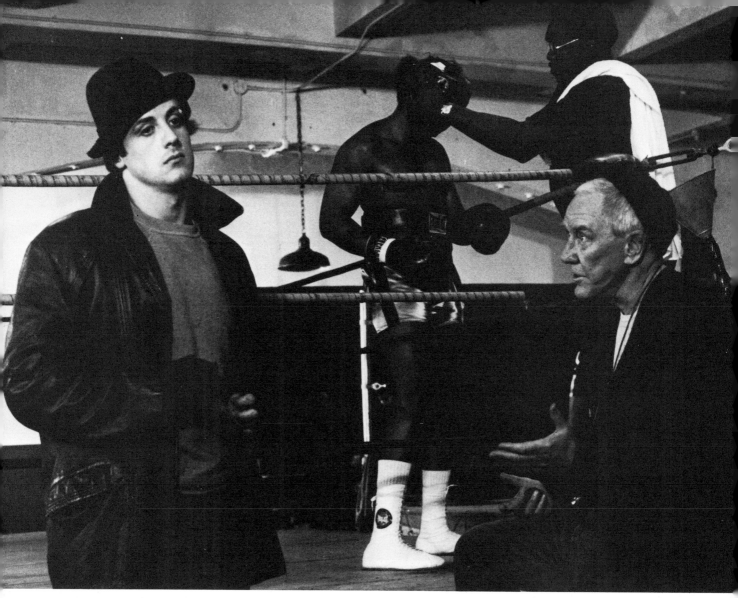

Mickey tells Rocky to retire.

Right: Rocky telling Mickey he's no bum.

You meet some nice
guys at the gym.

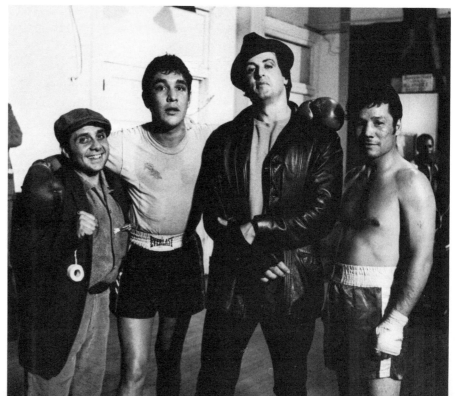

Trying to cope with the flu during training scenes.

Make-up man Mike Westmore giving Burgess Meredith a haircut.

Trainer Jimmy Gambina taping my hands before a sparring match. Producers Bob Chartoff and Irwin Winkler are in the background.

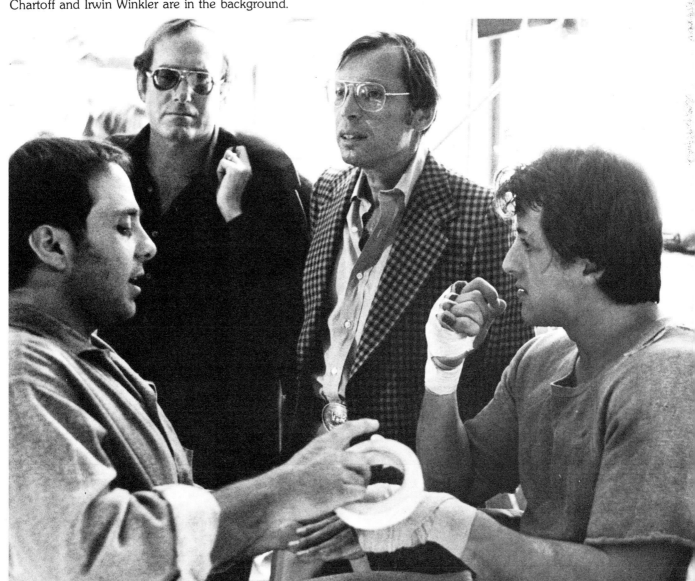

Rocky getting in shape after many hours banging the target gloves.

Preparing to do stomach work with Jimmy Gambina.

This scene nearly destroyed my innards.

Mickey clocks his fighter on the speedbag.

Right: Rocky in practice clothes and fighter's stance.

Burgess telling Rocky to change his shirt.

The champ tries his charm on Miss Liberty.

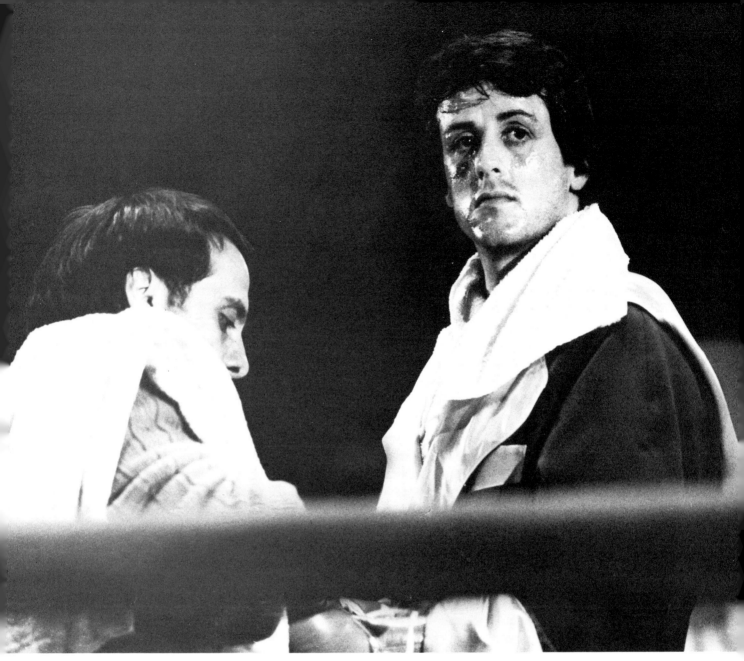

I'm watching the champ floating to the ring.

Rocky stalking Creed in
the first round.

73

Rehearsing the camera for the first round.

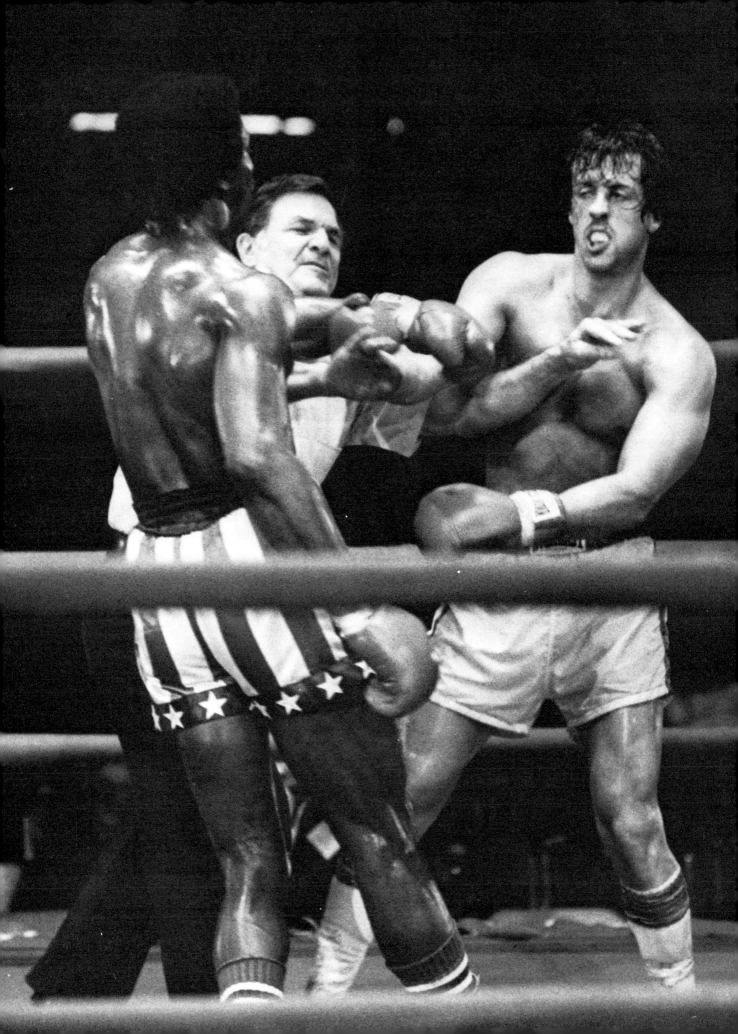

Above: The fighters being filmed by the revolutionary steady camera.

Below: Rocky stalks the champion as the camera stalks Rocky.

Rocky's attempt in the final round at winning the fight.

The fighters collapse in each other's arms.

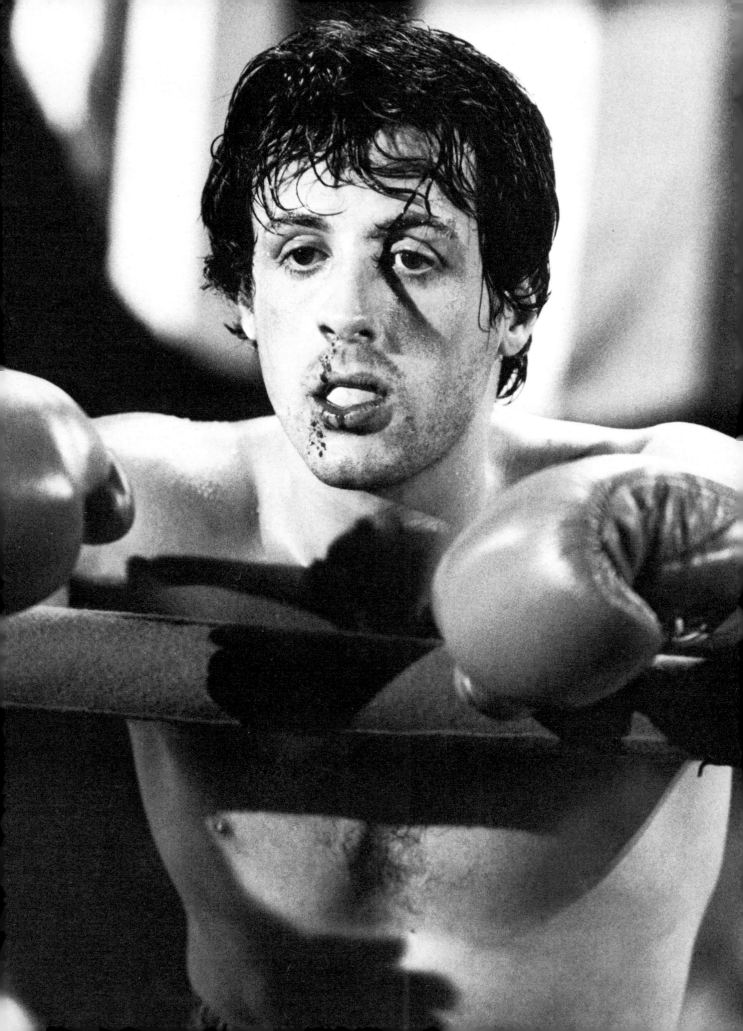

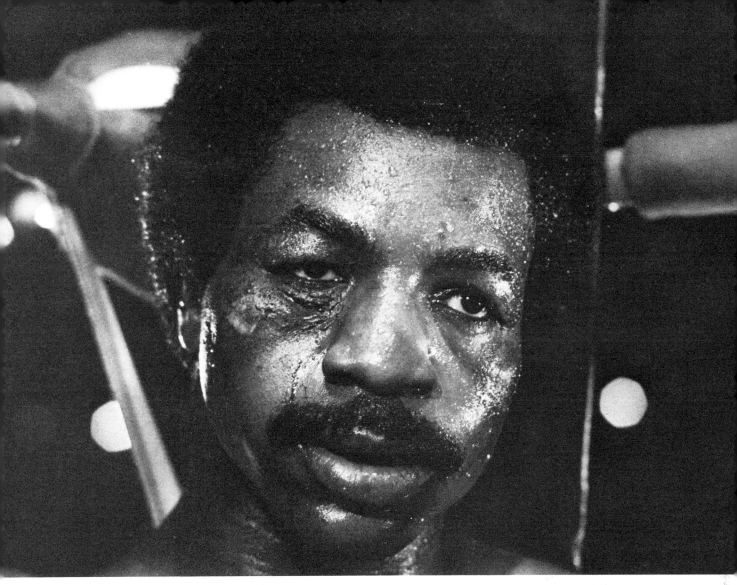

Apollo realizing he is in the fight of his life.

Left: Rocky bewildered after
first-round knockdown.

Rocky returning Apollo's punch.

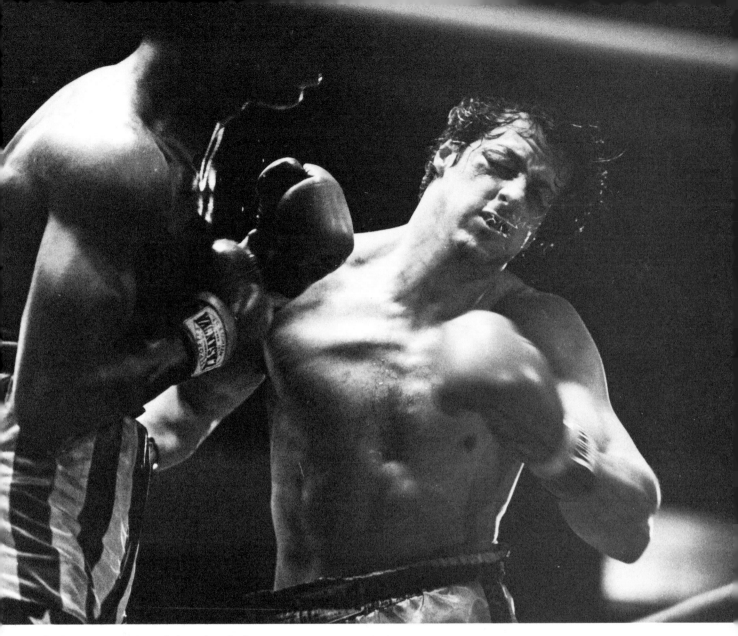

Carl giving me a month-long headache.

This proves all the punches
were not misses.

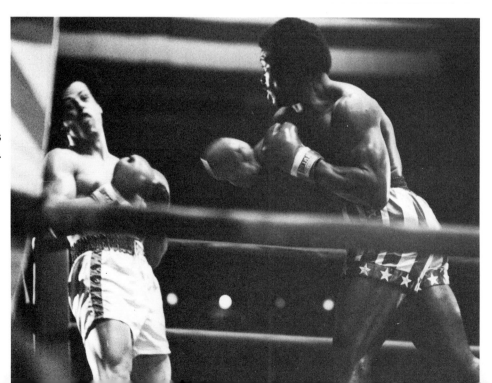

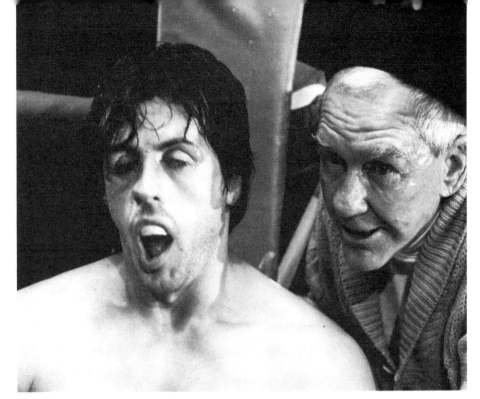

Rocky gulps air between rounds.

A 100% kidney punch.

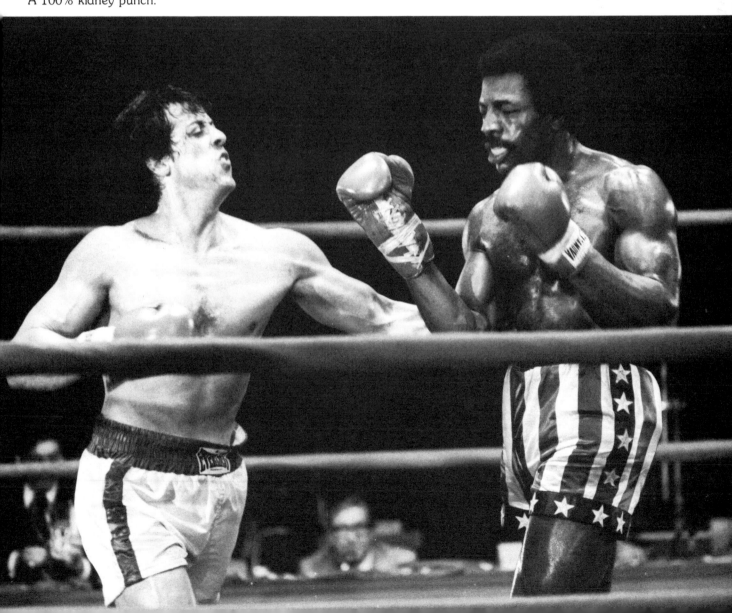

Rocky helped to his corner after shattering Creed's ribs.

Right: Rocky is beyond pain.

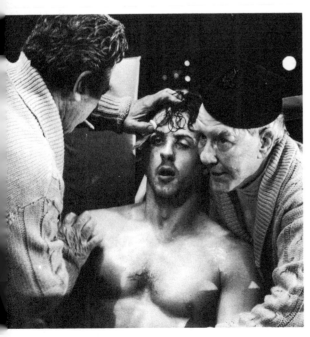

Rocky getting eye lanced. Mickey instructs.

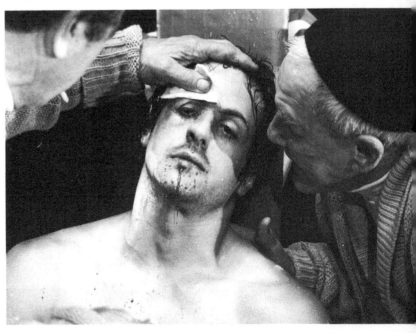

Lancing Rocky's eye in the fourteenth.

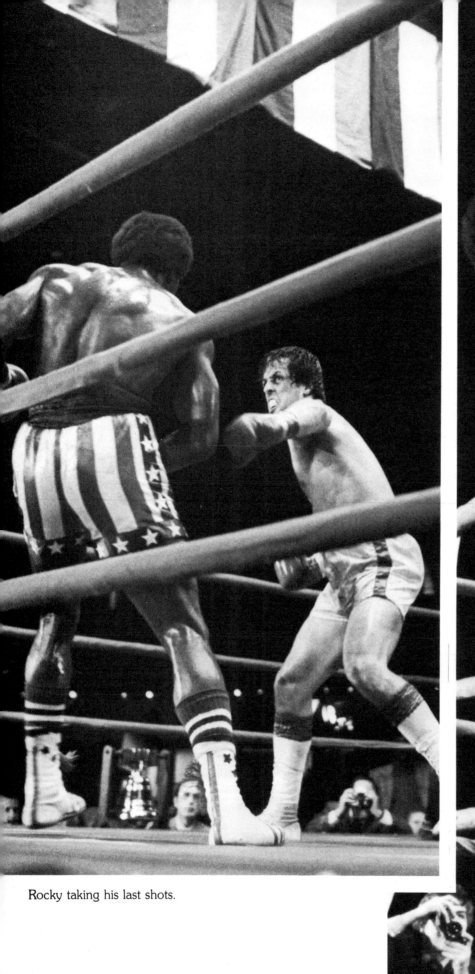

Rocky taking his last shots.

Creed's ribs are broken.

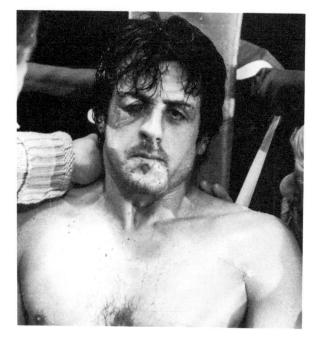

Rocky determined to answer the bell for the fifteenth.

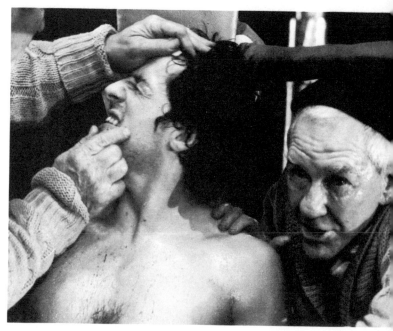

The trainer cracks an ammonia capsule.

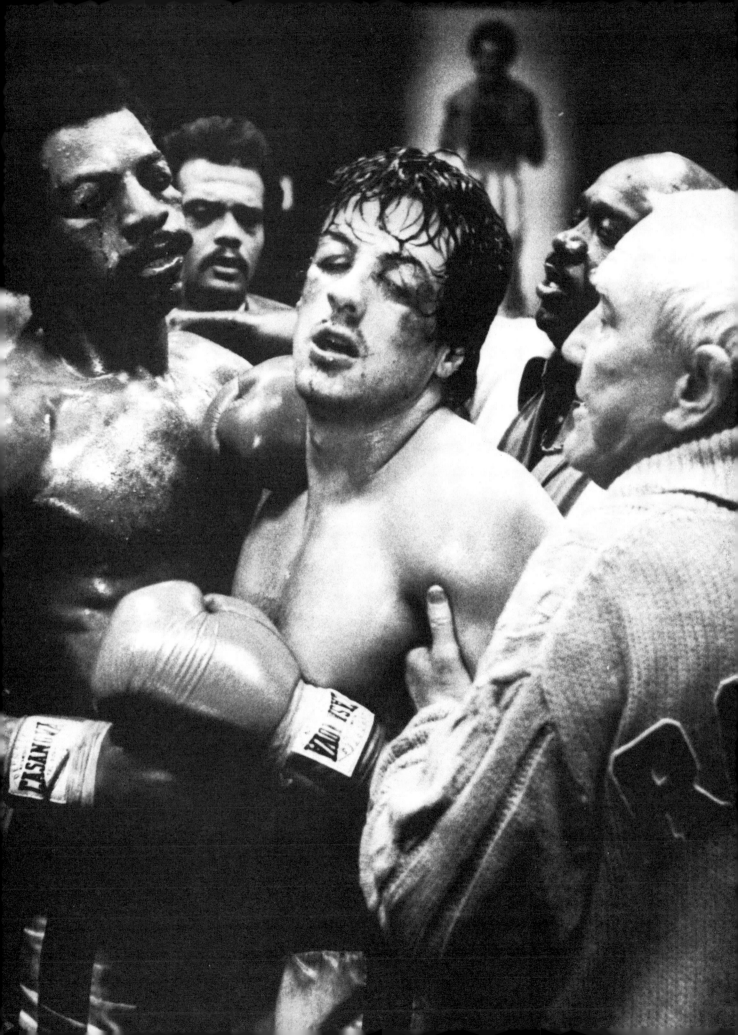

Rocky and Apollo.

Rocky and Adrian after the
fight (a scene never used).

Joe practicing his body punching.

Frazier is surprised that Carl is in such good shape.

Right: Carl and I overdoing for camera.

Executive producer Gene Kirkwood and I smile at
the end of the movie—we knew it was special.

ROCKY wins Best Picture at Academy Awards.
Robert Chartoff (right) and Irwin Winkler (left).

Overleaf: Moments after production ended.